Michael Alan grew up in West Sussex and after finishing his private education had a career in banking before a massive change into the world of horses, competing to a high level. Divorce led him to change once more into estate agency before completing his working life in a successful career in financial services, travelling to Brazil, Borneo and Zimbabwe. Now retired, the writing of this book provided him with great therapy and emotional release.

Tigger dedicates this book to his adorable wife, Wen, who has given him so much support in life, and to cousin Mary from his REAL family. I love you all.

Michael Alan

A BOY NAMED TIGGER

AUSTIN MACAULEY PUBLISHERS™

LONDON • CAMBRIDGE • NEW YORK • SHARJAH

A CIP catalogue record for this title is available from the British Library.

ISBN 9781398450974 (Paperback)
ISBN 9781398450981 (ePub e-book)

www.austinmacauley.com

First Published 2022
Austin Macauley Publishers Ltd®
1 Canada Square
Canary Wharf
London
E14 5AA

Early days in the snow at Horseshoe Lodge

There are few books, to my knowledge, about adoption. Those that have been written may not be of a biographical nature that tell the story of a little boy who started life so happy and then one day that happiness was torn away so dramatically, almost in a blink of an eye. I have written this book now as those who were involved with my early upbringing and adoption have passed away with the exception of one person – Mim. Life is what you make it – one often hears and in my own case my early life had a great bearing on who I have become.

I hope all who read this book will enjoy it, but also make YOU better people in the way you treasure your own family and friends.

What are the first memories of your life and how old were you? An interesting question and one that may well test YOUR memory. Some memories are vivid, others hazy, but in writing this book it certainly has refreshed many good and not so good times.

Tigger was a bouncy, loving little boy, who only wanted someone to love him. Life was a bundle of fun, just like him. He enjoyed life to the full and was with people that loved him as one of the family – until one day all that was to change.

Tigger was the name the Casewell family gave me. I guess because I was always on the go and bouncing around!

Auntie Peta in the middle – with Mim on the right

Chapter 1
In the Beginning

For Tigger, life could not have been much better – playing in a big garden, living in a house full of large rooms. They were truly joyous times and ones that he would remember forever and treasure in his heart. His mother – or so he thought – was a person called Auntie Peta. He was none the wiser at that very early age that you did not call your mother Auntie!!! She had two children, Miriam – Mim – and Mark, who Tigger assumed were his brother and sister. His father was a man he rarely saw as presumably he was out at work all day but a jolly man. Now Auntie Peta was THE most lovely person, like a big cuddly teddy bear who never seemed to get cross and was always happy. Mark and Miriam were quite a lot older than Tigger but they often played in the garden with him. He remembered the winters were often cold with plenty of snow on the ground and they all had great fun playing in this white stuff! Summer months were often spent down on the beach as a family, Mark and Mim helping Tigger to make sand castles.

Sitting on Auntie Peta's knee in front of a roaring fire was so relaxing. It seemed to be the most natural thing in the world to do, Mark and Miriam reading a book and father the newspaper. Bedtimes were also full of stories that filled his mind with imagination. Could life be any better? So very British and so perfect, so blissful. This was indeed the age of innocence and happiness. Could Tigger have been happier and more contented?

Tigger had arrived at Horseshoe Lodge, the Casewell's family home in Warsash as a babe in arms and the Casewell's were hoping eventually to be able to adopt him into their family. He was treated as one of the family, anyway, so it seemed the most natural thing to do. Life was not easy for the Casewell's. It was just after the Second World War and like most folk they were trying to get back on their feet. They had a big house to maintain and with two children of their own to bring up, money was tight, but Auntie Peta was determined to add Tigger to their family. How he came to be there he did not know, but at that age he was not to know that Auntie Peta was not his mum. This was his home and this was his family. However, things were to change – so, so dramatically.

Chapter 2
Devastation

Tigger was about three years of age and one morning Auntie Peta told him that they were going on a journey in her car. In his little world Tigger could sense all was not well. Auntie Peta was not her usual happy self. No, she was not cross with Tigger, but she was just not happy. They were about to go on a journey that was going to change his little life forever. He was none the wiser as to what was in store and they set off on the journey to Worthing. It seemed to take an age to get there, but when they eventually arrived it was to another big house. The house belonged to a Mr and Mrs Thomas. When they entered the house Tigger had a feeling of great uneasiness. By this time Auntie Peta was crying and she told him this was to be his new home and that Mr and Mrs Thomas would look after him. The feeling inside Tigger was one that he would take to his grave. His room was small and narrow with a very high ceiling. This was to be his bedroom whilst he was there. He did not know about such things but it was a guest house and he lay in bed and cried all night. The Thomas's were very anxious at Tigger continuously crying as they had guests staying and they were fearful that they would not appreciate a young child crying all night.

What in the world had happened to Tigger?' Why had Auntie Peta – his mum – gone away? Why was he at this place – Worthing? He could not ask, other than cry out for Auntie Peta. It must have been very distressing for the Thomas's. He was, however, there for a relatively short period. One day he was told to go down to the front gate where a lady was waiting for him with an ice cream. This person was his 'real' mother. But he did not know that at the time. That was the first and only time he was to meet his birth mother.

Tigger's real father was in the Army, the Royal Army Medical Corps. He and his mother had married just before the war and on his return Tigger was born on April 19th 1945. He was born in Guys Hospital London, his parents living in an affluent part of London. As it transpired, his father had met a German woman in Suez, Egypt during his service and as a result his mother and father separated soon after he was born. It must have been very traumatic for Tigger's mother, having his father return from the war and then a sudden separation. Tigger's father was now Camp Adjutant in Colchester – he was a career soldier. His mother was living in London, now pregnant and about to be separated from her husband. She had to support herself and therefore, for whatever reason, ended up in Worthing working as a receptionist in an hotel. In those days with no support it became impossible to look after a new-born baby as well.

Tigger was initially looked after by his mother's sister down in Devon. It was her sisters intention, and wish, that he should stay within the family and be adopted by them. Unfortunately her husband, Tigger's uncle, would not hear of it. He ended up at Horseshoe Lodge with the Casewells. How that came about we will never know.

So there he was in Worthing meeting this lady who meant nothing to him, but later he was to learn that this was her 'Goodbye'. How dreadful it must have been for her to never ever see Tigger, her little Michael, again. To make matters worse apparently there was only a very small number of the family who knew that Tigger existed. There was, in those days, a sense of shame to give ones child up for adoption. Tigger had wondered for a while when he was older whether he was indeed illegitimate, but no, he was not.

His little mind was in a complete state of distress. He was with people with whom he did not know, did not particularly like and he craved to be back 'home' with his family. What had he done to deserve this? What was going on and how long was this nightmare going to last? Things were to get worse.

Tigger lost track of how long he was at the Mill Road Guest House but it was apparent that whilst the Thomas Family felt sorry for him they could no longer be expected to give him a home. Tigger was to move on yet again. This time a little further down the road to Goring by Sea to a family called Stuart-Witton. A fine house, well-furnished and kindly people. But yet again he had not a clue who they were or why he was there. Bewildered beyond belief he just coped on a daily basis. On a Sunday it was off to church to a place called Rustington – a Christian Science church and whilst the Stuart Wittons were in church he was in the Junior Sunday School being looked after by more complete strangers. Remember this church as many years later a hair raising occurrence happened at this place!

Again Tigger had no recollection of the length of time he was at the Stuart-Wittons but unbelievably again he was to be

14

on the move, but this time it was to the couple who were eventually to be his adoptive parents.

Tigger was totally unaware of the plans for his future and come that fateful day his spirits were elated when who should turn up at the Stuart-Wittons but Auntie Peta. As you can imagine there were floods of tears and his little mind told him that at last he was going HOME and this dreadful nightmare would be over. How wrong was HE? His clothes were packed into a small suitcase and put in the boot of Auntie Peta's car, an open top sports model. Auntie Peta tried to explain in the nicest way that he was to go to a new permanent home as that was the wishes of my real mother and father.

"But YOU are my mother?" Tigger cried.

"No, I was just looking after you," she told him.

So much confusion and so much information for a little boy to absorb in such a short time that it was all like a very bad dream.

They said their goodbyes to the Stuart-Wittons and set off for Tigger's new Home. How Auntie Peta was feeling he could not imagine, but she had looked after Tigger for three plus years and now felt it was her responsibility to take him to people who were to adopt him. There had obviously been negotiations and meetings going on. Apparently it was the wish of Tigger's parents that 'he must go to people that can provide him with a private education'. No hint of a family who could provide him with love, as well. After about twenty minutes they arrived at a bungalow by a railway station – Angmering Railway Station and the place that was to be Tigger's new home – Woodstock, Angmering Way. As they drew up to the place two people came out to greet them, Christine and Bernard. Auntie Peta took Tigger by the hand

and introduced him to these two people who were to be his mother and father for the rest of his life.

Chapter 3
Tigger's New Parents and Family

"Hello, Michael, I am your new mummy and this is your daddy."

Tigger looked at Auntie Peta who had tears in her eyes. The agony she was going through must have been unbearable. It was years later that Tigger was to read a letter which told the real story as to how she felt. Tigger loved that woman with all his heart and now they were to part and he was not to see her for some time. She kissed and hugged him, got into her car and was gone. Tigger was all alone, or at least that is how it felt. Again strangers who he had never met, were to be his guardians, his parents. He felt desperately unhappy and sick to the core.

"Come along, Michael, come inside and see your new home and your bedroom."

He was taken inside this small dwelling – a bungalow, firstly into the kitchen, hallway and then a room that was to be his bedroom. Small but basic, clean and tidy. He had this uneasy feeling about Christine, Bernard was OK.

Christine was a small woman with dark short curly hair and a slight humped back. She was not a good looking woman and did not have a warm friendly or loving demeanour. Her real name was Clarice but was known as Christine. Bernard on the other hand was tall and slim and quite a different character which Tigger warmed to.

He spent that first night mostly crying and did not get much sleep. It was his dad who went into Tigger's bedroom to try and comfort him and he felt some solace from his compassion for him. And so it was to be. Woodstock was where Tigger would remain and Mum and Dad were now to be his parents. Little did he know in his innocence that at this time the authorities had no knowledge as to what was going on and he was living with his mum and dad in an unofficial capacity. This was 1949 remember, can one imagine this being allowed today? The days and weeks passed and Tigger gradually got used to being with this couple, Mum and Dad, who, to him were quite elderly, but they looked after him well, fed and clothed him and Mum gave him such a 'smarmy' hair style, which even at that age he disliked.

"Bernard, they have let his hair grow so badly – I have to do something about it!"

Tigger does not seem too happy about his 'new look'

His first inkling that Mum was a strange woman in many ways was after a child's birthday party that he had been to. He was still upset at being parted from his 'real' family and had eaten all manner of things at the party and upon being brought home by one of the parents he felt violently sick. Instead of being taken to the bathroom his mum said,

"Don't let him be sick in here, let him be sick over the drain outside."

She was obviously quite cross at a child making a mess, which made Tigger feel even worse. A good start to things!!! Not having had any children of her own, she seemed completely at a loss to know how to deal with the situation.

So to bed and another day completed and another night of sobbing!

Tigger had presents given to him by neighbours such as colouring books which he loved to fill in. His mum noticed that he was holding the crayons in his left hand which seemed to be the normal thing for Tigger to do.

"Bernard – have you noticed that he is using his left hand to colour in?"

"I hadn't noticed that – but what of it?"

"We cannot let him carry on doing that – when he goes to school they will call him names!"

So with that she always tied his left hand behind his back to encourage him to use his right hand to write. He eventually got used to that but from then on Tigger did various things with either his left or right hand or foot. He would throw a ball with his left hand, kick a ball with his right foot, bat with his right hand when playing cricket but left hand when playing racket sports! Even on occasions being able to swap hands during a game! Later in life he was convinced because of this he had become dyslexic, but was never tested. He always found examinations of any kind difficult to pass because his ability to hold certain information, he felt, was restricted – he much preferred to be shown how to do something rather than have to read complex instructions.

Dad was an avid amateur photographer and was keen to take as many photos of Tigger as he could. He made a lot of his own equipment, lighting, shades etc. He was very particular as to positioning, lighting so he would get the best possible results. During one photo session Mum really shouted at Dad for taking so long over taking the photos.

"How long does it take you to take a few photos?" she stormed.

It was not long before Tigger was in tears again. He still has photos today of that session where it is obvious for all to see that he had been crying.

Life became a series of ups and downs and quite stressful for a little boy to cope with considering his lovely life at Horseshoe Lodge!

Living next to the railway was exciting for a little boy and he would spend hours waiting for the trains and shouting out that he had seen a 'dinner train'. In those days the London trains had Pullman cars.

April was Tigger's birthday and he had a lovely treat. A blue tricycle with a little boot at the back where he could put 'things'. He became friends with the local neighbours and was soon a regular sight pedalling up and down Angmering Way. One of the neighbours, The Newmans, had a daughter, Joyce. She was drop dead gorgeous and Tigger was sure he was in love! She took him shopping with her on a Saturday, which he always looked forward to – Joyce taking him out!

Bernard – Tigger's new dad – a lovely and good man

Mum and Dad had the local grocery shop opposite to where they lived so he was able to cycle up and down the road in complete safety. He did little jobs in the shop to help his

Mum and Dad. It was just after the War so things were still tight and there was rationing, but Dad did well in the shop. Biscuits tins were displayed open to entice customers to buy, and when Mum was weighing out the biscuits, if the customer had a child she would always give one to the child – but also remember to take one OUT of the bag being weighed!

One of Dad's customers was a tall man called Mr Androvenda, who was a kind man and took a great interest in Tigger.

Mr A – or now to be known as Uncle Mike was to have quite an influence upon Tigger's life and a person Tigger was to have a great affection for. He was a tall upright man. Always with short cropped hair and spoke with a very educated accent. Very much in the mould of the once famous French actor, Charles Boyer. For the time being he was just a customer of Dads. Tigger's father was new to being his own boss, but had met Tigger's mother when they both worked at the Coop in Leicester. His father had given him some money to start up his own business and for some reason Tigger's mother and father came down south and settled in Angmering where they had just started this new business after the War. Uncle Mike worked on the London Stock Exchange and, having a good knowledge of finance, helped Tigger's father with advice on running his business and the right investments to make on the stock market. Having also just arrived on the scene he not only took an interest in Tigger's well-being but helped with the process of completing the adoption, which was to take around nine months.

On the beach in Sussex

Having come to the South from Leicester in the Midlands Tigger's parents' relatives still lived up there. Tigger's mother and father had their relatives all living close to one another. None of them had been introduced to Tigger, so a visit up there was duly arranged. Father had a Flying Standard car – FCD 292 – funny how that number had always stuck in Tigger's memory. During those days there were no motorways so the journey took about six hours or so. By the time they arrived it was dark. Tigger, understandably, was a little nervous wondering what his new 'relatives' would look like. Grandmother lived in a village called Swithland, just south of Loughborough, in quite a big house. She was quite a tall, big lady but with a kind face and demeanour.

"Well, here he is, Mother," Mum said.

That was the introduction to my grandmother. A big fire roared beside a cooking range in the large kitchen. Old fashioned chairs were around a good sized table and a rocking chair and a dresser with various plates on display. They had a good, plain meal and soon it was to bed. But where was the bathroom? Yes outside to a wash room and an outside toilet at the end of the yard. Up to bed by candlelight as there was no electricity upstairs. Tigger lay in bed thinking and watching the lights of the occasional car coming down the road and flashing its lights around the room. Tigger had a good feeling about this place, although he was still in a state of confusion – sleep quickly followed. Normally a child would have got to know grandparents from birth, but he was put in at the deep end, having to get to know a new family at the age of four!

Tigger felt like a goldfish in a round bowl with these, mostly old people, staring down at him. So who were all these new people? Well, there was Aunt Annie and Auntie Beatrice. Auntie Annie was one of Gran's sisters. A plump, grey-haired lady with a very kind and caring disposition and quite maternal, and a spinster. She and Beatrice lived together in a little stone cottage next to Gran's house. Beatrice was the daughter of Uncle Alf, Aunt Annie's brother, who had died some time ago. Tigger felt an immediate unease about Beatrice – Beattie as they called her. A bit of a 'dame', cold and clinical. Tigger felt like he was an outsider to her. Then there was Aunt Evelyn and Aunt Phyllis. They lived in a big, posh stone cottage up the road. They were both directors in a large hosiery factory in Leicester – Luke Turners. They were undoubtedly the wealthy ones in the family. Aunt Phyllis was not a relation of the family but was Aunt Evelyn's partner.

Evelyn was the brains of the whole operation and always wore men style pinstripe suits. She was to spoil Tigger rotten. They had two King Charles Spaniels, Jimmy and Charlie. Poor old Jimmy had something wrong with his mouth and his tongue always hung out of his mouth. They, as well, were spoilt and always went to work with the two aunts.

Swithland was in a lovely part of England and all the properties there had to be constructed in the local stone and slate. One of the few places outside Wales that had blue slate. Next to Gran's was a farm owned by the Walkers. Pleasant folk who allowed Tigger to spend time on the farm later when he spent wonderful holidays with Gran. Just up the road was the Charnwood Forest and in the spring it was blue with bluebells and the air was filled with that lovely fragrance.

Dad's family lived about five miles from Swithland at Anstey which was nearer to Leicester. Tigger was duly introduced to that side of the family. There was Dad's father. An averaged man in height, around 70 years of age, thinning grey hair, a moustache and rather deaf. Dad had two sisters, Madge and Margaret and a brother Arnold who all lived in the one-terraced house, entered via a central alley and we always entered via the back door. Tigger can never remember the front door, fronting the street, ever being used. He immediately had a good feeling about these people as well and so it was to be that they were always loving and caring and accepted Tigger immediately into the family as 'one of theirs'.

With the introductions to his new family over, in no time at all Tigger, Mum and Dad were back at Woodstock Angmering Way and back into the groove of the new family life. Tigger was still feeling pretty confused, emotionally

26

drained by what was and had been going on in his life. So much had gone on and so many new people he had been introduced to, in such a short time Then one day a big surprise. A car turned up outside the house and there was Auntie Peta. Glory be, she had come to take Tigger home. He watched as she came up the path with something under her arm. In a flash she was inside and throwing her arms around him. What bliss to be with the person he loved. The first person he remembered and the person he had always thought was his real mum. She had bought him a present as well, a green, handmade, wooden steam engine. Tigger loved it. But why had she bought him a present if she was going to take him home? Sadly it was not to be. After what seemed an eternity she had been 'allowed' to come and visit. Tigger was later to learn that Mum had ignored letters from Auntie Peta or any contact for fear Auntie Peta would try and take him back. He wished! There was another twist in that, which he was to learn of much later in his life.

Auntie Peta came and departed and life was again sad for a while. But there was a promise that Tigger would be able to visit Auntie Peta, Mark and Mim from time to time. Something to look forward to. Sometime later this did happen and Tigger was put on the train at Angmering, with the guard given instructions to keep an eye on him and then Auntie Peta met him at Portsmouth Harbour, over on the Harbour Ferry to Gosport and back to Horseshoe Lodge. How good was this to back on familiar ground with Mark and Mim. Tigger had a lovely day with them but in a flash he was back on the train and home. Such emotions to cope with at such a young age?

Chapter 4
The Move

Life at Angmering was much the same from day to day with not a lot happening and Tigger gradually got used to his new home, surroundings and his new mum and dad. It was his belief that children should never have preference between their mum and dads but that was in an ideal family environment. He definitely preferred his Dad. Mum and Dad were as different as chalk and cheese and one wondered how such different people could have got together, let alone married. They say opposites attract, but to Tigger, even then, that was carrying it a bit too far! Dad was a very placid man and Tigger never knew him to lose his temper. Mum on the other hand was a person who often made him feel that he never knew where he stood with her. Mood swings or what. Well she was in her mid-forties at the time so it was assumed the 'change of life' thing had a great influence with her odd behaviour! But at that age Tigger was not aware of such things.

Christmas was fast approaching and Dad seemed to spend a lot of time in a room where Tigger was not allowed in. He thought it strange but in his little world he thought it was something to do with his photography. But come Christmas morning all would be revealed to the mystery behind what was going on in that room. Intrigue! Mum and Dad were very busy in their shop on the run up to Christmas and Tigger was getting quite excited as to what Father Christmas would be bringing for him this year. His first Christmas with his new mum and dad.

There was a lot of activity on the run up to Christmas and then Christmas Eve. Tigger was in bed early as Father Christmas would not be coming until he was fast asleep. He was very excited. Then it was Christmas morning and Father Christmas had been and there was a big pillow slip at the bottom of the bed. It was obviously magic as Tigger had not heard a thing. Lots of presents from aunts and uncles. Pencil sets, colouring books and chocolate gold coins and some money from Auntie Peta. Mum and Dad were up and about and Tigger rushed out excited to tell them Father Christmas had been!

"He's also bought you another present," Dad said. "Come into this room."

The room Tigger had not been allowed in for so long. WOW – a train set. And what a train set. A full layout with a station modelled on Angmering Station, a lake, a bridge, hedges, fields, cows and sheep. The train was a brand spanking new blue Sir Nigel Gresley Hornby 00 Gauge, with three coaches. This was the best present Tigger could imagine. He had loved watching the real trains going past Angmering Station and to have his own model railway layout was the best thing. Dad was very artistic and had made the layout so well and Tigger was to spend hours playing with the set and adding to it over the years. He was truly happy and it made him take his mind off the sad days of the last year. He gradually accepted his new mum and dad and this was his home now. Until one day they were all on the move up to Leicester.

Dad had sold the shop. Tigger was to find out some years later that adoption had a certain stigma attached to it in those days and there were rumours that got back to Mum and Dad that he may be illegitimate. It got to them and so it was time to move on. They were to live at Grans for a while and Mum and Dad would have to find jobs again.

They were to live with Gran whilst Mum and Dad found a new place to live. Tigger loved his Gran. She was, as previously said, this large cuddly person with whom Tigger never had a cross word. Whenever Mum was in one of her moods or snappy, Gran would always comfort him and made him feel secure. He loved cuddles and being in her home. But he did miss stories at bedtime that he always had at Auntie Peta. Mum and Dad had met at the Cooperative Society shop in Leicester where they both worked, so that was the first place they went back to try and find work. They were successful, Dad being employed on a full time basis and Mum part time during the afternoons. Tigger would have been five years of age by now and so they had to find a school for him. This was to be one of those pre-school places in someone's large house on the Leicester Road just outside Leicester. Tigger was put on the bus outside Gran's house – one of Prestwells coaches and dropped off right outside the 'school'. He enjoyed it there, soon settled in well and had fun with the other small group of children.

Mum was obviously worried about money, work and what their next step would be and her concerns manifested themselves in the only way she knew how and that was nagging about the most silly things, and goodness knows why, but she made Gran's life a misery at times too. She was a bully. Tigger did not like this atmosphere and felt quite miserable at times. Life was not like it had been at Horseshoe Lodge. School was only part time and Tigger left each day around lunch time to catch the bus back to Swithland and arrived back around half an hour before Mum left for her afternoon shift at the Coop. It was quite often a miserable half hour and Tigger was pleased when Mum left for work and the rest of the day he would spend happily with Gran. On occasions Tigger would miss his bus home from school and imagine the delight when he saw his Mum's bus going in the opposite direction to Leicester as he was waiting for the next bus home to Swithland. He did not have to endure the half hour with her nagging! What a start in life! Mum had things down to a fine art by being quite different when both her and Dad came home in the evening. Butter would have melted in her mouth! 'What a Jekyll and Hyde,' Gran had said to Tigger. He did not really understand what she was saying and this saying would come back again many years later!

Time passed and Christmas with Gran came and went. Gran loved Christmas and made a big thing of cooking the turkey, stuffing, bread sauce and proper gravy from the turkey fat. She had made the Christmas Pudding and cake weeks earlier. None of the turkey was wasted, down to making turkey soup from the bones! It was a strange existence living with Gran but Tigger liked it there because it was in the country and he could play with one or two other children and in the brook – catching Bully Heads, small fish from under the stones and in the fields opposite her house. However the stay there was to come to an end. Dad had found another business in Anstey, just down the same street where Grandad lived. It was a corner grocery shop with the house combined. And so they were on the move again. Dad knew the grocery trade inside out and did very well. Many of his customers knew him from when he lived in Anstey as a boy. Tigger did not like this new home as much as being with Gran. It was in a town, but he soon made friends with a few other children. There was a cinema opposite the shop and the folk who ran it had a boy around Tigger's age and they had great fun during the holidays running around inside the empty cinema. There was also a Junior Saturday Cinema Club which was great fun with good films, cowboys and Indians and cartoons.

Tigger was getting to know his extended family of aunt and uncles and grandad very well and although Grandad was deaf they both communicated well. On lovely sunny days he and Tigger would go on walks across the fields to Bradgate Park. They loved it there and Tigger was, in the years to come, to spend a lot of time having fun days there. It was a very large park with a herd of fallow deer, a ruined house, a brook with many waterfalls, a hill with two monuments on the top, one of which was called Old John, a stone structure shaped like a beer tankard.

The ruined house had been the home, briefly, of Lady Jane Grey, the nine day queen of England before she was executed. After her execution all the oak trees in the park were also beheaded and to this day one can still see evidence of that. The stream provided boys with the pastime of stickleback and crayfish hunting and Tigger would often bring the little fish back home in a jar hoping they would survive to keep as pets! When Grandad and Tigger went to Bradgate Park it was across fields where cows grazed and Tigger took great delight as Grandad strode out picking up his leg and plonking it straight on to a cow pat! He knew what was going to happen, he was sure but he just let Tigger do it knowing it would make him laugh. Tigger was at his happiest when he was away from his Mum. How sad.

Chapter 5
The Grand European Holiday

They stayed in Anstey for some time and Dad must have been making quite a success of the business and earning quite bit of money. They were to have their first big holiday. A foreign holiday no less, touring France, Italy and Switzerland. They set off in the Flying Standard and they were to take Aunt Madge and Margaret as well, plus all their luggage. They travelled down to Dover to catch the Cross Channel Ferry. Of course no roll on roll off ferries in those days and the car had to be loaded by crane. They were all excited and looking forward very much to seeing places many people in those days only dreamt of. Even Mum was quite excited.

In what seemed no time at all they were in France. Dad had planned the holiday well with all the necessary maps from the AA and places they would stay. Dad seemed to get used to driving on the "wrong side of the road" very quickly. It seemed quite strange. As they trundled along Tigger was very interested in all the old buildings and the countryside and kept them informed as to what they should be looking out for. 'A cemetery on the left,' he said and everyone burst out laughing. He did not think it was THAT funny. They stayed overnight in a small guest house. Strange sleeping away from home.

Mum, Dad and Tigger in one room and the aunts in another. In the morning they were off again and speeding down the French country roads. Then all of a sudden they were overtaken by a car wheel. What the heck is that, where did that come from? Crunch!!! It had come off the car and from the side Tigger was sitting! Dad managed to control the car very skilfully and they ground literally to a halt. Yes a wheel had come off the car! Well you can imagine, the mood changed very quickly.

"I thought you had checked the car wheels before we left England!" Mum screamed. "Now look at the mess you have got us into."

Dad then picked up the car wheel and proceeded to hunt back up the road for any wheel nuts they could find. Tigger had little idea what he was looking for but helped as well. But to no avail. A kindly French man stopped, not being able to speak a word of English nor any of them being able to speak French, but he took Dad to a local garage and eventually suitable nuts were found and they were on their way once more, albeit with a buckled wing. Mum of course changed the mood of the holiday completely by keeping on about it, bringing the aunts to tears, until one of them had the nerve to tell her to shut up otherwise they would be going back to England. Anyway silence reigned. But silence was better than Mum nagging.

Onwards through France and down to the French Riviera to Nice where they stayed in quite a plush hotel where the charming proprietor insisted on calling Tigger 'Little Meekal'. His aunts were fairly young so were completely charmed by him! How wonderful it was to see oranges and lemons actually growing on trees. Dad was in his element with his camera and took loads of photos – which, for Mum, was far too time consuming at times! From France they went on to Italy and again nice hotels and charming people. So soon after the war British tourists were a little thin on the ground. From Italy they then went to Switzerland which was truly magnificent. The car struggled up and down mountain passes often having to stop to let it cool down and top up with water. And snow like you have never seen it. Wow, Tigger loved snow but in some places where machines had cut through the road the snow was much higher than the car! At one mountain pass where Dad hoped to be able to drive the car over, a workman stood in the road, stopped us and jabbered away to him in 'foreign'. Dad did not seem to understand what he was trying to tell him. Mum got very impatient and they all thought, *Here we go again.*

"Can't you understand, Bernard? He's telling you we cannot drive ahead anymore! What's the matter with you?"

Unpleasant atmosphere immediately created! Dad had to turn around and go back to the railway station where he had to put the car on the train and they all went through the pass on the train and through a long tunnel – the St Gotthard Tunnel. So exciting going on a foreign train AND through a long tunnel. Eventually they disembarked and carried on their journey arriving late at Wildersvil just outside Interlaken (between two lakes, Thun and Brienz) staying at Hotel Belmont owned by Madame Zbinden. Hotel Belmont was an imposing building sitting on top of a small hill overlooking the main village of Wildersvil. Steps led up to the entrance leading into a large lounge with a small bar snuck into a corner. Large picture windows on either side of the lounge gave views to the mountains and to Lake Brienz. The corridor straight through led to the conservatory dining room. The wide stairs to the first floor bedrooms were adorned with Swiss memorabilia of wooden skis, sledges and shovels.

The following morning everyone was up bright and early to a lovely day and it was then that they could really appreciate the magnificent views. The view was directly up the valley to the really high mountains of the Alps and in particular The Eiger, Monch and Jungfrau – all above 11,000ft high. Dad was very careful to check the car over, wheels, oil and water before they set off on their first day in Switzerland exploring and taking in the breath-taking scenery. By this time, fortunately, Mum had calmed down and appeared to be joining in the enjoyment of the holiday.

They explored the village briefly. There was a small railway station with one track leading one way down to Interlaken and the other upwards to Lauterbrunnen. Another track led to the botanical gardens up the mountain to Schynige Platte via one of the original old trains. A wonderful panoramic view from the summit.

They set off up the pass to Lauterbrunnen – the Valley of the Waterfalls where there is a most spectacular waterfall that cascades over the cliff ending up almost as spray at the valley floor. This particular waterfall is often featured on calendar photographs. They parked the car and then took the train up to Wengen and then up to Kleine Scheidegg at about 9,000ft. Here one can see the glaciers of the huge mountains of the Eiger, Monch and Jungfrau, the blue ice clearly visible glistening in the sun. One can continue up the mountain and through the tunnels of the north wall of the Eiger, disembarking at the Jungfrau at 11,333Ft. One of the features of this rail journey is that there are two stations within the north wall. The train stops and passengers walk through tunnels to a viewing area. The first station has the most spectacular window views out of the mountain looking towards Grindelwald and the surrounding mountains. The drop from this viewing point is thousands of feet. The second station takes one to views over a glacier high in the mountains with beautiful blue ice – indeed most spectacular and beautiful. The top of the mountain called, The Top of Europe is one of the most spectacular views. From the station within the mountain a short tunnel walk takes one to the other side of the mountain which overlooks the enormous Eigergleicher Glacier which snakes its way down towards the Italian side of the mountain. The air is very thin at this height and walking is at a very slow place. Returning to this inside of the mountain, a lift takes one up to a weather station from where one can see both sides of the mountain and with views onwards and upwards to the majestic Jungfrau.

After a while and many photos taken they retraced their way back down the mountain, back to the car and continued their exploration of this beautiful country, meeting locals and trying on the traditional Swiss hats and jackets. Madame Zbinden at Hotel Belmont had been the perfect host and made the stay so much more enjoyable. We made our sad farewells and it was time to return to the UK and Anstey with many happy and not so happy memories, but even at that young age Tigger made his mind up that if the opportunity arose he would return to Switzerland and in later years his wish came true.

Chapter 6
On the Move Again

Life continued to be somewhat mundane with Mum's mood swings up and down. After about eighteen months or more they were to be on the move once more. Tigger guessed that Dad had an offer on his business he could not refuse, as they say, and they returned to Sussex to yet another business venture just to the west of Worthing – on the corner of Northfield Road and Littlehampton Road. A true corner grocery and provisions shop. Once again having to settle and getting used to a new home. They lived above the shop, as they say, bedrooms and a lounge upstairs and a living room and kitchen downstairs, with a middle room where there were loads of boxes – Dad's store room for his shop. There was also a good sized garden. Tigger liked the garden and was soon growing his first seeds there. Peas and beans and a sycamore tree. His mum had bought the peas and beans and told him she would help plant them. But Tigger was impatient and wanted to plant the seeds himself. So he dug this big hole and the seeds went in! After a few days his Mum told him she would come into the garden and help him with the seed.

"Oh I have already planted them in that hole there!" said Tigger.

"That is not how you plant peas and beans, you stupid boy! Why could you not wait for me – what a waste of money!"

Tigger felt dejected. He had tried, he thought his Mum would see the funny side of what he had done. Anyway, they dug the seeds up and planted them properly in a long line. They grew well and a fine crop of peas appeared.

Time for Tigger to go to his first 'proper school' – Miss Kayes Broadwater Preparatory School set in its own grounds on the corner of Thomas a Becket cross roads. He soon settled in well mixing with the other children. He enjoyed it and was soon going to and from school by himself. What independence! Miss Kaye walked with a limp – why Tigger did not know, she was a jolly individual and she made them all feel happy. She always called the children, 'little rats' if they were cheeky or misbehaved. Something Mum totally disapproved of but Tigger guessed in a funny way it was a term of endearment!

Tigger did well at school and received good marks which DID please his Mum. He also did well at sport. There was not a lot of room at the school for much of a playing field but they did do running and jumping. At the end of term there was prize giving which all the parents were invited to and Mum came along. Names were read out for various awards and the boys received presents – mostly toys. Tigger wondered whether he would receive a prize. He hoped he would, especially as Mum was there. YES!!! Tigger's name was read out and he was expecting a big present, maybe a lovely toy. But no it was just a very small red box. He opened in front of Miss Kaye.

"You should be very proud of this, Michael, I have made you school captain and that is a solid silver crest that you can pin to your blazer so everyone will know who you are. Well done, Michael. Your mother and father should also be very proud of you."

Really, Tigger thought. He would have much preferred a nice toy like most of the other boys. But at least Mum was pleased. If Tigger could do something to please her that was good, it would keep her in a good mood. He often asked Mum if she was in a good mood, which, ironically, often put her into a bad mood. Tigger could not understand that, so he soon learned to say nothing. As prize giving was the end of term that meant something called a report was sent to parents. This duly arrived at home and Mum and Dad were very pleased to read that Tigger had a glowing report. One more term and it was summer holidays.

It was difficult for Tigger's Mum and Dad to have much of a holiday as they had the shop and could not afford to close the shop for any length of time, so they had to take short breaks to visit the relatives in Leicester. Tigger's Mum had sort of an obsession with making sure doors were locked and taps were turned off properly which Tigger knew really got on Dads nerves and he was determined to break her habit of standing at a door continually trying the door handle for an eternity to make sure it was locked. He did succeed to a degree. But his limited success was to come back to bite him in a big way!!!

They were all ready to set off to Leicester for a few days break over a bank holiday. Mum and Tigger were in the car waiting for Dad, when a neighbour caught him just before he was about to get in the car.

41

"Oh, Mr Warrington, I have run out of butter – please?"

Back in the car Mum said she would check the shop door to make sure it was locked.

"Don't be silly, Christine, the door is locked."

Off they set for Leicester, Mum in a bit of a mood, but soon everything seemed OK. They always went to Leicester the same way and Tigger's dad thought it would be good to go another way, through a place called Henley.

"Why have we got to go a different way? You will get lost. If we do not go our usual way I am getting out."

Mum was getting hysterical. Tigger had never seen Mum quite like this before and became quite scared.

"Bernard, turn round and go our usual way!"

"Calm down, Christine, I know exactly where we are going. I thought it would be good to go a different way for a change."

"Well I want to go our usual way – turn round now or I am getting out."

How could she get out when the car was moving? Dad carried on, when all of a sudden Mum opened the car door as the car was travelling along.

"Christine, what the devil do you think you are doing?"

If she wants to get out, let her, thought Tigger – she's a nutcase. Reluctantly Dad turned around and they travelled to Leicester their usual route – in silence. Tigger was quite upset by all of this – it was a new experience for him.

When they arrived at Grandmas, Mum was sweetness itself as if nothing had happened. In a quiet moment with his Dad, Tigger asked why Mum had done that in the car on the way up.

"Try not to worry yourself about it – she is going through a funny stage."

As if he was supposed to know what that meant!

Tigger, his Mum and Dad had quite a nice time up there chatting to the aunts and then to Anstey to Grandad and Aunts Madge and Margaret on Saturday afternoon.

Sunday came and there was a knock on Gran's door. A policeman stood there.

"Is there a Mr Warrington staying here?"

Dad went to the door.

"Hello, Officer, what is the problem?"

"Do you own the corner shop in Northfield Road Worthing?"

"Yes."

"It seems you came away without locking the shop door and our officers down there have found customers wandering around the shop."

Well, you can imagine. All hell broke loose with Tigger's mother. Gran tried to calm things down, by saying, 'These things happen!' Tigger had never heard such language from his mother and he felt so sorry for Dad having to endure such an onslaught of abuse. The holiday was cut short and soon they were all back home to the shop. The door checking returned with a vengeance! Life for Tigger was quite unpleasant for a while until eventually things returned to some sense of normality. Oh for the tranquillity of Horseshoe Lodge!

Chapter 7
A Change of School

During the summer holidays Tigger's Mum and Dad took him
to another school to meet the headmaster and to have a talk.
It was a lovely school. An old mansion with what seemed
miles and miles of playing fields.

Goring Hall was to be Tigger's next new school. A private
school where Tigger was to start his education with 'proper'
lessons. He was taken down to Worthing by Mum to a big
store called Kinch and Lack. Tigger had never been in a shop
like that before. Upstairs was where school uniforms were
sold and there Tigger and his mum were to first meet Mr Mac,
as he was known. Tigger never knew his full name. It could
have been McIntosh, McIntyre or any Mac you could think
of. Mum was insistent on personal service. So it was to be.
Grey flannels twice, white shirts twice, one blue blazer with
gold braid, one tie and one cap, one leather satchel.
Remember the TV series – *Are You Being Served?*

"This is your new school uniform, Michael, you look after
it as it cost a lot of money," Tigger's Mum told him.

The first day of the term at Tigger's new school came. Up
early and on with the new uniform. Photograph taken by Dad
and it was then off to Goring Hall in Dad's delivery van.

Exciting stuff, meeting his new teachers, meeting the other boys and learning new things. Dad dropped Tigger off at school where they had been welcomed by Mrs Boulton, Tigger's form teacher. She was a nice smiley person with whom Tigger warmed to immediately. The entrance door to the school was big and opened to a large hallway and sweeping stairs to Tigger's classroom upstairs. Most of the children in Tigger's class were also new to the school and soon new friends were made. Names exchanged and stories told. Many of the boys – at this all boys school – had brothers, and some were at Goring Hall. *Oh for a brother or even a sister,* Tigger thought.

Mrs Boulton was to take many of the lessons, although there were one or two others who took nature study and gym. The headmaster was a Mr Cornish and he and his wife lived at the school. They were a very pleasant couple and although neither of them taught Tigger he did meet them from time to time. Tigger liked the school, soon settled in well and was starting to do well in his lessons which he liked very much – especially nature study. He also got on very well with Mrs Boulton and even at that young age, Tigger secretly fancied her! At the end of the first term Tigger had a very good report which pleased Mum and Dad, so all was well in the house.

Terms came and went and Tigger was gaining in confidence. He continued to receive good reports which pleased his Mum and Dad. He began to get some pocket money and he was allowed to spend some of it in Dad's shop. The sweets looked inviting, particularly the pink nuggart, but his Mum soon brought him down a peg or two by telling him that was not good for his teeth.

Well why sell it, then? thought Tigger. The school had an Open Day when parents could go to the school, meet the teachers and discuss their sons' studies. Tigger and his Mum went along together – his dad had to work in the shop and he had glowing reports. Parents were able to visit their sons' classrooms to see artwork they had done and the star chart and Tigger was top of the class in stars. Mum had a long chat with Mrs Boulton. On the way home Tigger's Mum said she was very pleased with his progress although Mrs Boulton had told her he was, at times, getting a little too 'big for his boots'.

Huh, why would Mrs Boulton say that? thought Tigger. After that Tigger didn't fancy her so much anymore!

One day Tigger had done something 'naughty' at school and he was given a detention – his first ever. He was very upset. Would his Mum find out? What would the punishment be? It turned out to be not so bad. Instead of being able to play with his friends at play time he would have to meet up with Mrs Cornish in her garden to help her do some weeding! Tigger liked gardening so it was not much of a detention. Tigger liked the school. He liked his lessons. In fact there was nothing he did not like about school life at Goring Hall. He liked play time when he and his friends could go out into the large playing fields and explore the woods around the school and the ditches when it had been raining! He was told off at home when his 'expensive' shoes were wet from his playing! End of another term and a good report – except for one detention and yet more moaning from Mum.

Life was pretty good for Tigger by now. He was doing well at school and enjoying his time there. He had a new girlfriend, Wendy, who lived opposite them in Northfield Road. She lived with her Mum and Dad and sister Shirley.

Wendy and Tigger got on well and often played together. Mum and Dad worked hard in the shop and the business seemed to do well. But Tigger's Mum had bouts when she would be really grumpy and picked on Dad and continually moan. Tigger used to go out with his dad in the delivery van calling on his many customers with their 'orders'. One day Tigger was in deep thought about his mother. He was aged about seven. He felt he could talk to his dad and he plucked up the courage to ask his dad.

"Why can't you take Mum to the doctors, because she is always in a bad mood and moaning at you? Surely a doctor would be able to cure her?"

"If only it was as simple as that, Son – don't you worry yourself over it."

"But it is so unfair on you all the time."

Even at that young age Tigger knew that this was not a normal mum – not like Auntie Peta!

Poor old Tigger had such mixed feelings. Sometimes his Mum was as nice as pie then, in what seemed an instance, she changed. At times he felt he was treading on eggshells!

Tigger was enjoying his time at Goring Hall School and imagined spending the rest of his school days there. This was not to be. One day his mum and dad sat him down for a chat and his dad said that they did not think that his current school was going to give him the best education, so they were looking at changing his school. They would take him to another school – Shoreham Grammar – where they would have a chat with the headmaster, a rather large tubby man, very similar to Capt Mainwaring in the TV series *Dads Army*. They were all given a tour of the school and decided whether it would be good for him to go there instead of Goring Hall.

The school looked OK but was not as grand as Goring Hall, nor did it have playing fields like Goring Hall, these were further down the road. The playing area was just a large gravelled area, again not so good as Goring Hall. But it was not down to Tigger whether he went there, it was his mum and dad who were to make that decision. Anyway it was only early spring and Tigger could not go to this new school until September so there was plenty of time for any decisions to be made – or so he thought!

Tigger quite liked living over the shop and there was the garden he could play in and Wendy was across the road so any thoughts on moving did not enter his head. However, one weekend his mum and dad drove over to a place called East Preston, which was a village next to Rustington where the Christian Science Church was. They arrived at East Preston to look at a piece of land with a couple of ponies grazing on it.

"Well this looks OK, eh, Christine?"

"Yes, I suppose so – but can we afford it?"

Well what was that all about? Tigger thought.

It turned out that his mum and dad wanted to put some real roots down. Buy a plot of land and build their own home on it. A bungalow.

A few weeks later and on another visit they could see that the builders had already started work, the foundations were in place and walls were being built.

Regular visits were made and arguments between Tigger's mum and dad as to room sizes, what was to go where etc etc. Pretty boring stuff to Tigger. Then one day some good news. Tigger's mum was to go up to Grans to visit for a while and it would be just Tigger and Dad. Tigger felt so much more relaxed in Dad's company. Dad and Tigger made several visits to the bungalow. The roof was on and flooring was going down. The bungalow was now really taking shape. Uncle Mike lived just around the corner from the bungalow and they often met up with him.

Tigger's Mum eventually came home and when she found out that Tigger and his Dad had been regularly to the bungalow without HER she went berserk! Dear, oh dear, what was the matter with the woman?

"How dare you go without me and make decisions without consulting me?"

"The builders needed to know what to do and how to alter things which were not right. I could not wait for you to come back."

On and on she went and she really did make life unpleasant. She even had 'a go' at Uncle Mike. He just told her to grow up and if she was his wife he would put her over his knee and give her a spanking – as she was behaving like an overgrown child. She did not speak to him for weeks, not that he was bothered!

The bungalow seemed to be finished in next to no time, Tigger, though was not that happy as his room seemed very small. The corner shop was sold and the move to the bungalow was completed. Everything smelt new, there were plenty of trees around and there were three other new homes next to the bungalow. New surroundings and another new home for Tigger to get used to.

Chapter 8
The Bungalow

For Tigger's parents the opportunity to buy a piece of land and to build a bungalow – a brand new home was the pinnacle of achievement for them. They had both come from rather poor backgrounds with parents who had to count every penny and work very hard for it. They had started their working lives working in the Coop in Leicester and had progressed their lives with monetary help from Tigger's grandfather and purchased their own businesses. They had always lived over or near their businesses so to have their own place away from where they worked was a great feeling. A real sense of achievement. They had been unsuccessful in having children of their own, so relatively late in life, they had decided to adopt and this is how Tigger came into their lives. Tigger's mother was 47 years of age and his father younger by 9 years at 38 years of age.

The bungalow was set on quite a large plot and with Tigger's Dad's artistic flair, plans were made to design a beautiful garden. The bungalow itself was not all that large to begin with. A lounge, dining room, one large bedroom and a quite small one – Tigger's and a kitchen. The bungalow was later to be extended to incorporate a lounge/dining room and an extra bedroom. There was also a detached Marley style garage.

Dad had great plans for the large garden which in its current state was little more than a field. The land needed to be fertilised. During winter storms a lot of seaweed was washed up on the beach. So down they went in the van with loads of bags. Gosh it did smell, but after many visits the garden was covered in seaweed – it smelt like the sea! The garden was dug and a variety of vegetables were grown. Potatoes, cabbage, carrots, in order to break down the soil. With the plans completed, eventually, things started to take shape, a large lawned area, a magnificent weeping willow tree, flower beds, a veg plot and an area set aside for a greenhouse. The main feature was to be an ornamental fish pond with a bridge over, a rockery and two small ponds which had waterfalls cascading in the main pond.

Tigger loved working in the garden with his father. Many visits were made to various local garden centres and nurseries supplying ornamental trees, Cherry almond and even peach trees were purchased along with a wide variety of ornamental flowering bushes. The front garden was laid to lawn, also a rockery, a stepped path to the front door and a driveway to the garage with a rose arbour over. Spectacular when all the American Pillar roses were in full bloom. Flowers and rows of tulips standing like soldiers adorned the bedded areas. It certainly was a picture and one that many folk who passed by stopped to gaze upon. The bungalow and the gardens were complete but would provide continued work during the long summer evenings and at weekends in order to maintain a very high standard of care. Tigger was expected to do his share of the work as well!

Now the shop was sold and Tigger's dad had no job to go to, he set about finding new work. The next town was Littlehampton and it was there that Tigger's dad was to work for the next few years. Three shops in a row, a fishmongers, a butchers and in the middle a grocery shop – all owned by a local wealthy businessman. Dad was to be the manager of this middle shop and he relished the task of getting this run down business back on its feet and with his wealth of experience it did not take him long to make many changes. The man who owned these three shops was impressed by what Dad was doing and gave him a free rein to do what he liked and one of those things was to create the first delicatessen in Littlehampton.

Tigger's dad set off for work on a bus at 7.30 in the morning leaving Tigger around half an hour with his mum before he too set off for the station to catch the 8.19 London train where he would travel to his new school at Shoreham. Only on the first morning did his Mum take him to the station. He picked up his season ticket from the ticket office and waited on the platform for the train to arrive. He was aged eight so it was a brand new experience for him not only to go on a 'London train' but to travel by himself. The train duly arrived and there was a mad rush for a seat. The train was crammed full of city gents in bowler hats, pin striped suits who carried briefcases and rolled umbrellas. He knew no one and at first it was all a bit nerve racking. Not talking to anyone but listening to all the talk from these men. He noticed that there were one or two other boys on the train wearing the school uniform. A black blazer with school badge, grey shorts and grey shirt, house tie and a black school cap with a white patch in the middle. Tigger stuck out like a sore thumb in his brand new clean uniform and a blue case for his school books, pens and pencils. The case had been bought for him by Auntie Peta. He was aware these other boys were talking about him.

"Bet he's new?"

He could hear them say that.

The train arrived at Shoreham and Tigger strode excitedly to Pond Road and to Shoreham Grammar School, the school he was to spend the rest of his school days. An imposing Victorian building of red brick greeted him and following the other boys Tigger found himself in the reception hall when a master was calling out for 'new boys' to gather 'over here'. Tigger's name was ticked off on a list and a senior boy was told to take Tigger to his classroom. Through the hallway and out through a door at the end into the first glimpse of the playground, an uninspiring mixture of tarmac and gravel. Turning right past a long wooden building, which was the school laboratory, and into a smaller playground, a sort of annexe to the main area, and then onwards to a detached building in a corner with a corrugated tin roof.

"This is your classroom – go in where you will find your form teacher Miss Brady."

With that the boy was gone.

Inside Tigger was greeted by Miss Brady, a plump, red haired, bespectacled woman who spoke with an Irish accent.

"Welcome, Warrington, find yourself a desk, sit down and wait."

The desks were old and many had previous boys names engraved with a pen or dividers spike. There were also some crude messages as well!

Several other boys were already sitting at their desks and Tigger found one next to one of the other new boys.

"Hello, my name is Tigger – well actually it's Michael but I am known as Tigger."

"Hello, my name's Johnny, I am new here as well."

And so began a long friendship with Johnny that was to last beyond their school days.

After the formal introductions by Miss Brady and the giving out of the school lessons timetable for each day, they were introduced to school prayers and assembly. Once a week certain classes would attend morning prayers in the school chapel across the road and in the other week classes would attend morning assembly in the senior classes – classrooms were divided by partitions which were drawn back for assembly.

The school chapel was a proper little church with pews, an altar and organ which was air driven by a boy pumping the air in via a wooden handle whilst the music teacher played the hymns.

Tigger's first impression of the school was completely different from Goring Hall. Yes it was a different type of building and there was no grass playing field, but it had an air of being a 'proper' public school. It would take him some time to get to know new boys, new masters and a new type of education. Goring Hall seemed more of a family affair. Shoreham Grammar was much more business-like. There were more pupils there and certainly more boarders. Tigger was soon to find out that the boarders thought they were far superior to the day boys. The teachers, though, were not a bad bunch at all.

Tigger's first day seemed to be over in a flash, so much to get used to! Tigger's train left Shoreham at 4.04 p.m. and as school finished at 4 p.m. it was a bit of a dash down to the station.

One of the many instances recalled by Tigger was the rush for the train. Firstly the master of the lesson had to finish bang on 4 p.m. in order to be able to run the four minutes to the station to catch the train. Secondly, on many occasions the boarders in the class knew the boys who wanted to catch the train so they would either hide the satchels or cases of the boys in question or their school caps. The said articles would then be returned after about two or three minutes, knowing then that it would leave no time to catch the train! The next train was twenty seven minutes past four so Tigger would be late home.

Johnny lived at Worthing so both he and Tigger shared the journey. *It was good to have someone he knew and it was a good time to get to know Johnny a little more,* Tigger thought. Johnny had a younger brother Martin and an older sister Frances and his father owned a big furniture store in Worthing.

"See you tomorrow, Johnny."

The rest of the journey to Angmering did not take long and soon Tigger would be telling his mother all about his first day at his new school.

However, Tigger's mother was a person who ran her life to a strict routine. Being expected home on the 4.04 p.m. train she would have Tigger's tea waiting, washing up would be done and then father's tea would be prepared. BUT if he was late it put all this routine out and she was really put in a bad mood. Late for tea, late for washing up, late for dads tea etc etc. Dad did not mind at all – but then sometimes Dad was late so that really put the cat amongst the pigeons!

Chapter 9
Getting Used to His New School

Tigger had to get used to his new school pretty quickly and be aware of his new surroundings, certain boys and a different type of teaching. One of those things that was different was corporal punishment. Miss Brady was the most strict teacher he had come across in his short time at school. He had wondered why she always carried a small square ended hardwood ruler. It was not JUST to draw a straight line. He was quite shocked when he saw it first used. One of the boys in the class had done something wrong so he was called out to the front of the class, told to hold out his hand and he received four sharp whacks with this ruler. Tigger could see from the boy's expression that it really hurt. Tigger had never experienced anyone having corporal punishment before. It was quite a shock!

Being a new boy many of them were keen to make friends and spend time with one another at 'play time' playing King He – a ball game, football or cricket depending upon the season. However as a new boy certain small gangs of boys were also keen on carrying out the 'initiation' on the new boys. This involved being held pretty roughly, frog marched to the 'cold tap' and being ducked under until all the boys hair was soaked which inevitably meant the shirt and blazer – unless of course the 'new boy' was smart enough not to get caught. And that gained respect. Tigger was determined not to get caught. He could not bear the thought of being roughed up and then having to sit through lessons feeling wet, as well as going through a grilling from Miss Brady. Tigger was getting wise to these little gangs and so was Johnny. At play time they were always on the lookout for anything suspicious going on and eventually always managed to give them the slip, until they gave up and respect was recognised.

Tigger, Johnny and another boy, Piers became good friends and spent most of their time together during break times at school and also sat at desks close to one another. Tigger enjoyed his lessons and Miss Brady took a variety of subjects but also there were one or two male teachers that took nature study, music and woodwork. Miss Brady continued to be very strict and although the boys gave her respect she was by no means their favourite teacher. Canings were regularly dished out until it became Tigger's turn and, yes, it did hurt, it really hurt. More of the boys were becoming more and more annoyed by these canings. One day Miss Brady had to go out of the class for a short meeting and she made the mistake of leaving her cane on her desk. A big mistake! Now the classroom – Form One had a loft space above the boys desk area and the access space was open, so one brave lad, Nichols, who had had his fair share of Miss Brady's cane, took the stick and with one quick and accurate toss it disappeared up into the loft never to be seen again. This was all a new experience for Tigger and he thought it was great. On her return Miss Brady asked if anyone had seen her cane.

"No, Miss, you did not bring it into class," they all said.

And she never replaced it. Future punishment was with a twelve inch ruler which was far less painful. What a result!

School at Shoreham became very good for Tigger. He had made some friends, enjoyed his studies and received excellent marks.

The school was quite strong on sport and had quite good facilities for its time. The sports ground and gymnasium were separate from the main school and were situated around half a mile down the road – a ten minute walk. Physical training was one of the lessons held once a week and games for one whole afternoon. This was the first school that Tigger had experienced x-country running, a sport which he was to excel in. The autumn term was when football and x-country started. The changing rooms were very cold and everyone changed as quickly as possible. Tigger always enjoyed the sport times at his school and was disappointed if they were ever cancelled as a result of poor weather. Those times were usually taken up with book reading. These periods were taken by Mr Thomas – Poofy Thomas, as he was known. He was an ex-ballet dancer and could skip across the top of desks like a nimble monkey and clip a misbehaving boy in an instant. However he was excellent at reading and had the boys spellbound with his readings of Bulldog Drummond or The Hound of the Baskervilles.

At the end of his first term he was given a big brown envelope which was 'To be given to your parents'. On arriving home Tigger's mum opened up his report, a formal looking document with a black bound cover. After a while his mum turned and said,

"Well done, this IS a good report. Keep it up next term, we have sacrificed a lot for you to be able to send you to such a good school. It costs a lot of money. Do not let us down."

That was praise indeed from Mum! Tigger so much wanted to please his mum and dad and be loved, but still something was missing.

Tigger's early years at Shoreham Grammar were fun and in these formative years he was to learn much about life as well as in his studies. He was keen to learn. In general he liked and got on well with his teachers and continued to achieve high standards. He received praise from his parents but was continually reminded by his mother of the sacrifices that they had made to send him to a private school. Any subject that Tigger received poor marks for or a poor comment in his report, his mother would chastise him and tell him she expected better the next term. As the terms rolled by and school fees rose Tigger's mother had to find a job to help fund Tigger's education and this gradually put a strain, at times on relationships at home, with Tigger's mother moaning and complaining increasingly about things. Tigger began to feel uneasy. He had had such a turmoil in his life when he was adopted and he had taken some time to get used to his new surroundings and 'parents'. His mother was the sort of person who was alright one minute but the slightest thing seemed to turn her mood. Tigger was about aged ten when his mother started to work again and left home before Tigger went to school, so he was on his own for about half an hour before he left for the station. By then he was having piano lessons and so this time was spent practicing his scales and music pieces.

One day Tigger's mother sat him down for a chat to tell him a little about his past and why he had become adopted.

"Your mother and father separated soon after you were born and your mother did not want you. No one wanted you, your mother was not a very nice person and so when I heard about you I told the people that I would have you. I felt sorry for you. Your mother was a very good pianist, in fact she played to concert level and so I felt it was right that you should learn to play the piano as well. It costs a lot of money so I want you to do well so the money is not wasted – but if you ever want to find out about your parents or meet them then you will not be able to live here – we are now your parents and you are to have nothing to do with them."

A lot for Tigger to take in. Being aged four when he was adopted he could remember all about it so what his mother had said about being adopted was nothing new to him. He was rather shocked at what he had heard about his 'real' mother. He wondered what she was like, where she lived and whether he would ever see her again. It made him feel unhappy again.

Weekends were mainly spent tending the garden, even in the winter. A variety of vegetables were grown in the garden, potatoes, carrots, beetroot cabbages, beans and peas. The root vegetables were stored in barrels in the garage for use until the spring. Winter evenings were spent watching the TV and sitting by an open fire. TV at weekends in those days consisted of Dr Who – yes even then, a news programme, In Town Tonight and maybe a variety programme or comedy series. We sat having toast and jam or crumpets. Tigger's mother often sat him on her knee. Then on one such Saturday he was sitting on her knee and she was tickling his legs when gradually her hand rose up his legs, up and up into his pants and started tickling and stroking him. He did not know what to do but felt very uneasy at what was happening. Suddenly

Tigger's father put his newspaper down and shouted at Christine.

"What the hell do you think you are doing? Leave him alone."

"I am doing no harm to him and anyway he likes it."

With that Tigger jumped off her knee and sat in a chair and there was silence for the rest of the evening until bedtime. The same thing happened a couple of other times when Tigger's father was out of the room, until Tigger refused to get on his mother's knee ever again. These episodes continued to make him feel uneasy about his mother. He began to think she was rather more strange than he had thought.

Gran used to come down two or three times a year but always at Christmas. There was so much to do in preparation and Gran was a great help with the food. The bungalow was decorated throughout and Tigger loved to help doing this. Dad too was busy in the shop so often was late home. He was busy preparing his shop with Christmas Fayre and enjoyed being adventurous buying new products – especially as his shop was the only delicatessen in Littlehampton. He was very popular with the two shops either side of his and to his many customers. He had a flair for shop window dressing and this drew the customers into all three shops. His boss was particularly pleased with him. He was a modest chap who quietly went about his business and he was good at it. Oh for the days before the giant supermarkets! Tigger's mother, on the other hand, was far from calm and collected and whilst it was the season of goodwill, she became more irritable, flustered and bad tempered! Poor old Gran felt the sharp end of Mum's tongue regularly, but she took it all in her stride and never retaliated. At his age Tigger enjoyed Christmas and received many presents – obviously Auntie Peta NEVER forgot Tigger and often received a book voucher. Presents from the aunt and uncles in Leicester, neighbours and friends and of course his mum and dad. Christmas dinner was always a large turkey with all the trimmings. By this time in his life Tigger was introduced to the local church – Church of England, so he had to go to church on Christmas morning and every Sunday. One of the reasons he kept going to the church was that the local Private Girls School – West Preston Manor, had boarders and they also went to Sunday service and Tigger became friendly with one of the girls – Lorraine from Claygate! Letters were passed discreetly to and from each other, but the relationship never progressed!

Christmas Lunch was ready around 1.30 p.m. and the small kitchen was full of steam and fluster, but Dad calmly carved the turkey, whilst Gran did the vegetables – cooked to an inch of their lives and gravy, Mum made sure the Christmas Pudding was steaming away. Lunch over and all the washing up done and everything cleared away ready for 3 p.m. and the Queen's Speech, which in those days was around fifteen minutes in length. Mum always stood erect for the National Anthem and expected us all to do the same! The usual Christmas TV programmes watched and tea followed later by a cold turkey supper.

Winters soon passed and the longer days of spring and summer fast approached. Everything at this time was going well at school.

The school week at Shoreham was Monday to Saturday – with Wednesday and Saturday being a half day. Home in the afternoon unless you were chosen for school games practice, football in the winter, cricket and athletics in the summer.

Tigger was often chosen to represent his school House, Nelson, for football and athletics.

Sometimes on a Saturday he would get off the train at Worthing and meet up with Uncle Mike and have lunch at either Lyons Tea House or Roberts Denton Lounge on the sea front. He loved these times and was able to speak frankly with Uncle Mike and the concerns he had over his mother. It was all part of his education eating at such places which his mother and father never went to – in fact they had no social life whatsoever. The bungalow and the garden was their life.

During the holiday periods, especially the Easter holiday Tigger felt a bit lonely. Both Mum and Dad were at work and Tigger was left 'home alone'. Mum was home around 2 p.m. Tigger, though, was left with a list of jobs to do. Dusting around the house. Weeding and watering in the garden and woe betide him if it was not done to a high standard. More nagging from Mum. In the afternoons Tigger was allowed out to play with neighbouring children, climbing the trees out front and playing 'Cowboys and Indians'. During the summer holidays things were a little more exciting.

By this time Tigger had a new Raleigh bicycle, which he loved – freedom to cycle wherever he wanted. His friendship at school with John Scadgell was good and soon Tigger was invited up to his house for days. He lived with his parents, his younger brother and older sister right on the edge of the Downs. With little traffic on the roads in those days Tigger's parents thought it safe for him to cycle the six miles up to High Salvington where John lived. Tigger loved going up there, John had such a warm loving mother and he and John spent the days on their bikes cycling along tracks across the Downs, playing in old chalk pits and smoking woodbine from the bushes! John occasionally went down to Tigger's home but Tigger was always somewhat embarrassed by his mother's behaviour and questioning of John.

One day Tigger returned home from school with news that the school was arranging a holiday to Switzerland – Lugano – the Italian side and wondered if he did some jobs and earned some money, he could put his name down. Johnny was going.

His father found him his first holiday job at a local nursery where his father used to purchase produce for the shop. Church Farm run by a Mr Hovel. Tigger enjoyed the work immensely and began to save his earnings for the trip to Switzerland.

The holiday arrived and about 30 boys all gathered at the school for the coach trip to Dover. There was a lot of excitement amongst them all, the sea was rough and many of them were on deck to see the waves breaking over the bow. One of the boys, Gee, was to say the least, rather large and each time a wave broke they all crouched down behind Gee, and he wondered why he was the only one getting wet! The train journey across France and into Switzerland was pretty uneventful but nevertheless interesting and excitement continued to mount as they approached their destination. This was the first time that most of the boys had been away from home without their parents so the masters in charge had their work cut out keeping them all in check! The place they stayed was a sort of Youth Centre right by Lake Lugano with its own rowing boats the boys could use.

The holiday was really enjoyed by all with various trips up mountains, on lakes to visit villas and a day trip to Milan. John and Tigger enjoyed each other's company and bought gifts home for parents and even tried their first cigarettes! As usual time went quickly and they were on their way back home. Lots to talk about when they were back at school the next term.

Tigger's mother even moaned at him as they had not received a card from him – well, it takes time to arrive from abroad? The holiday gift was also not up to scratch either!

Other holidays were spent touring southern Ireland with his parents. Tigger loved a new experience and he enjoyed this, but the thing he most enjoyed was going up to Leicester to see Gran, aunts and Grandad. He was put on a train at Brighton by his mother who gave one of the stewards some money to make sure he kept an eye on Tigger. It was a fast steam train that went directly from Brighton to Leicester where Aunts Evelyn and Phyl would meet him in their 'posh' car. He would stay at his Grans, have fun playing in the fields and catching minnows in the brook over the road. One local lad had a bow and arrow, a proper one with steel arrows. They had fun seeing who could fire their arrows the furthest, they seemed to go miles. Part of this holiday was with Aunts Evelyn and Phyl to their holiday bungalow at Happisburgh in Norfolk. It was right by the sea, set high on a cliff with steps down to the beach. Maybe now this has been washed away over time? You could see for miles from this place. There were other children also on holidays with their parents. The area was quite remote and along the cliff tops were disused military war bunkers which extended for hundreds of yards underground and Tigger and the other children spent hours exploring and playing in these places. Luckily one or two had torches so they could see where they were going. They had 'battles' against one another, one side being British, the other the Germans!

This particular part of Norfolk had an abundance of fruit farms and Tigger and his aunts enjoyed going to these farms to pick their own raspberries and strawberries. On the way back to the bungalow thick fresh cream was bought to top off the fruit. These were lovely carefree days for Tigger and he loved spending time with his aunts who loved to spoil him. But all good things had to come to an end and soon it was back to Swithland, their home and then back on the steam train home to Sussex. A sense of foreboding always descended upon Tigger. Part of him did not want to return. He still missed his life with Auntie Peta.

Chapter 10
Life Gets Harder

After the summer holidays, it was back to school. He was by then in Class Lower 4A. There were two 'streams', 'A' and 'B'. Stream B was considered to be where the not so bright boys were. Tigger continued to do quite well at school but not with the 'brilliance' so often expected of him by his mother. Tigger was finding some of the new subjects – algebra, geometry and physics a bit of a challenge and rather boring as well.

The physics master, Mr Petherbridge, whose nickname was Dracula also did not help matters. His lessons were so boring! So why Dracula? He looked, poor man, as if all the blood had been drained out of his face, he had a slow drawn out voice and had an air of mystery about him. 'Hey boy,' was one of his favourite expressions. Far from putting the fear of God into the boys, the boys must have put the fear of God into HIM! They really did play him up by misbehaving in class. Poor old Dracula could not keep order. One of the pranks they did was, as they entered the laboratory they turned on all the gas taps and within minutes the smell of gas was terrible, they all ran out of the lab panicking and crying, 'Gas, Gas!' How they got away with such behaviour?

Although some of the times at school were rather uninteresting to Tigger he did enjoy his sport. The physical exertion expelled some of his increasing frustrations. He was better at the longer distances – 440 yards, 880 yards, the mile and x-country. he loved the winter months for the x-country and the school had a particularly challenging course. From the playing fields, across the main A27 road and up over The Downs towards the Beeding Cement Works, down through a farm and then back along the Steyning Road, off into some fields and then crossing three deep streams which fed into the local River Adur. Sometimes in January and February the ice had to be broken before the boys could go across the streams! Tigger loved it.

During the Easter holiday Tigger had his 13th Birthday and Gran had come down to stay. Tigger's school report was not up to his usual good standard in some of the subjects. His mother nagged like mad and his father was disappointed. One day when his father was at work Tigger's mother started on about his report, how bad it was. Every parent wants the best for their child and wants them to do well at their studies but Tigger's mother was obsessed with his work and if he slipped up in his studies there was hell to pay. That particular term Tigger had begun to tell lies about how well he had done, coming home telling his Mother how good his marks were, forgetting that his school report would tell a different story. So the nagging started and got worse and worse.

"Why have you lied?"

"I have not!" pleaded Tigger.

He had never felt so scared he feared something was going to happen. Gran pleaded with her to stop.

"Leave the lad alone."

"You keep out of it, Mother, it's got nothing to do with you."

Suddenly Tigger's mother went to the bathroom and started to fill the bath up with cold water and told him to take his clothes off. By this time poor Tigger was beside himself with fear. What was happening? Gran was crying, the bath continued to fill with water until it was near the top. Stark naked Tigger was forced into the bathroom and was told if he did not tell the truth he would be put in the bath and be drowned. Screaming and shaking with fear he did not know what to do or what was going to happen. This was probably the worst time in his life and he felt a great sense of utter despair.

"I want my Auntie Peta!" he pleaded.

"She won't help you she was glad to be rid of you as you were so much trouble to that family as well."

Suddenly and without warning his mother told him to put his clothes on, she pulled the plug on the bath and then inexplicably she gave him a hug and told him that was just a warning and never to lie again. Tigger continued to shake with fear and emotion and there was a terrible atmosphere.

"And do not tell your father when he comes home – I do not want him upset – you have upset enough people in your life."

Tigger's reports did not improve and out of fear he started to alter his reports – badly – to give the impression his marks were better than they were. '5s' were altered to '8s' and '1s' to '4s'! He was soon found out when the reports were returned to the school the following term and a letter sent to Tigger's parents. More moaning. Dad was really sorry that Tigger had resorted to doing this and even told Mother she had to tone down her nagging as Tigger was beginning to fear her. But Tigger's mother's reply was,

"We should never have adopted him. He is turning out bad, just like his mother. After all we have done for him, after all the money we have spent on his education and this is how he repays us, all the sacrifices we have made, the hours I have had to scrub floors cleaning for people. Lies and deceit is all we get from him. He will turn out to be a tramp, just like his mother."

Tigger really felt low. OK he had not paid attention in some of his lessons, but he did find great difficulty with some of his studies. He did not know what to do. He just wanted a cuddle and to feel wanted and loved. He would dread coming home from school and spending time alone with his mother. She often nagged him over the most stupid thing and get so wound up she would throw him out of the house in his bedroom slippers, in the cold and rain and then only call him back in when Dad was due home.

"Come back in and do not tell your Dad. I do not want him to know you have been upsetting me!"

Tigger was in the depths of despair. Life could not be any unhappier. Dad was no fool and he could often detect an atmosphere. Tigger often heard his Dad talking to Mum telling her to calm down and give it a rest.

For a while things improved and life was a little more bearable. It was the Easter term and Tigger was coming up for his fourteenth birthday and school reports were due.

Chapter 11
Breaking Point

It was springtime again and how quickly the year had gone by, Tigger thought his studies at best had improved and at worst were not bad! In Upper 4a the boys were allowed to see their reports before they took them home. Tigger opened his and to his horror his report was worse than he could imagine, he knew it would be bad, but not as bad as this! It was terrible and his mother would certainly kick off big time. He felt sick to the bottom of his stomach. He dreaded going home to face the music. He would have to wait about an hour and a half before his mother came home from work. The wait would be agonising. On the way home on the train his mind was going crazy. Then EUREKA, he had the solution. He would run away from it all. He had his new bicycle. He would get on it and ride away from all the troubles at home. He had spent some of his happier days lately on his bicycle so what better thing to do than get on his bike? He always kept it clean and well-oiled so it was ready to go. Swithland in Leicester, 186 miles away where his Gran lived did not seem far when he went with his parents in the comfort of a motor car.

Arriving home Tigger quickly gathered together a few belongings that he could take with him. A pullover, some socks and pants and most important of all, his Post Office savings book. He would need that to buy some food and drink on his journey – still it was only 186 miles! He had a large saddle bag on his bike and quickly he stuffed everything in, and was soon on his way, having left a brief note for his parents to say he could stand it no longer and was going to run away. He did not say where he was going. It was up to them to guess where he might go. The thing he feared most was getting onto his bike only to see his mother appear round the corner coming home from work. Phew! First hurdle over. He was on his way. He was free at last. That is exactly how Tigger felt. He had the whole world in front of him and he was on his way to Swithland in Leicester to visit his lovely Gran. Tigger was pretty fit for his age, doing a lot of training at school and cycling everywhere, so it did not seem to take long before he was going through Arundel and cycling up the long hill to the top of Whiteways Lodge and from there it was a lovely long hill, Bury Hill, downwards towards Fittleworth. On and on he went and was approaching Guildford along the A3 where he spied an AA Patrol Man standing next to his motorbike and sidecar. He was on his phone and Tigger was convinced he was speaking to the police about a missing boy. His mother would have long since arrived home and no doubt had been on the phone to his father telling him about Tigger's disappearance. Yes, it was bound to be a phone call to the police. So he sped by as fast as he could go and in the distance he dared look back, but the AA man was still there. False alarm. Strange that a young boy in his school uniform should be cycling along the A3 by himself. On he went spurred by this 'let off'. Through the outskirts of Guildford and on towards Bracknell. By 7 o'clock in the evening Tigger had arrived at Henley on Thames and the light was fading. After Henley there was a long hill to tackle up towards a little village called Nettlebed. Before the ascent Tigger needed to take a rest. He sat on a roadside bench wondering what was happening back home. Bet they were watching the BBC programme 'Tonight' hosted by Cliff Michelmore. He was beginning to feel lonely as dusk approached rapidly. Anyway sitting there would not get him any closer to Gran. Having taken his rest he tackled the long hill. Eventually he reached the top, it was completely dark and very tired. He had to take a rest so he pulled into a gateway and tried to snuggle down under a hedge. He put his pullover on and wrapped his school raincoat around him as best he could. It was cold. He was not comfortable but he must have dozed off because when he woke up the volume of traffic had died down considerably. It was 3 a.m. the stars were bright in the sky. He was even more lonely, a little scared and felt like crying. He could not sleep, so he thought there was nothing for it but to set off again. Little traffic meant a clear road and less chance of being spotted.

Having come up the hill after Henley, there was a long gentle hill back down the other side and through Nettlebed. He had a new Dynamo lighting system on his bike and the faster you went the brighter the beam on his light got. So, building up some speed downhill the light became as bright as a car headlight, faster and faster he went. Wow this was fun. He was enjoying this bit. He knew that at the bottom of this hill he had to turn right towards a town called Dorchester on Thames. He duly reached the right turn and off he peddled again at high speed. He did not recognise this bit of road. But, hey, it was night time and things tended to look different in the dark. After about two miles he came to an abrupt halt. in front of him was the entrance to an RAF Station – Benson. Damn. He had taken the wrong turning. So nothing for it but to turn back. The longest two miles of his journey. Back on the right road, he made the correct right turn and was soon passing through Dorchester.

The next big town was Oxford, and by the time he arrived there it was 6 o'clock in the morning and folk were up and on their way to work. Poor old Tigger was beginning to get some peculiar looks from some – what was this boy doing, on a bike, in a school uniform cycling through Oxford at 6 o'clock in the morning. Still no one stopped him and unbelievably he did not see one policeman. Having managed to get past Oxford unscathed, it was onward towards Northampton, some way off, but pretty level roads ahead. He had renewed vigour and felt strong and determined to arrive at Gran's without anyone stopping him. Finally he was cycling through Leicester City centre. He had remembered every single part of the route – apart from the unscheduled visit to the RAF!!!

Out of Leicester, up the Foss road to Anstey where his grandfather lived and then the final piece of the journey to Swithland. He could not believe that in 24 hours he had travelled on his bike for 186 miles without a hitch and was knocking on Gran's front door.

'Hello, me duck, you have arrived. Come here.' She gave him one of Gran's special hugs.

How good did that make Tigger feel? And then he burst into tears.

The police had visited Gran that morning to say Tigger had gone missing and to let them know if he should arrive in Swithland. It was doubtful as it was thought; he would try such a long journey – he would go back to Warsash and Auntie Peta. All police resources had therefore been concentrated in the Hampshire area. Thank goodness for that, thought Tigger. Gran quickly informed Aunts Annie and Beatrice. A phone call was made to the factory in Leicester to tell Aunts Evelyn and Phyl, then of course Tigger's parents and the police. The search was called off. Tigger had been found or at least, he had arrived! After something to eat and drink Tigger sat down for a well-earned rest. After a while his Gran started to ask him questions.

"What made you run away? What had your mother done to you? Were you scared? But you are safe now, we will look after you for a while."

Tigger did indeed feel safe now. His long journey was worth it and he had no thoughts about going back. He did not know what would happen, but his Aunts would sort something out.

Gran prepared Tigger a hearty meal and soon Aunt Evelyn and Phyl were home. Aunt Evelyn being an astute business woman calmly talked to Tigger about the situation and how it had arisen. This was a great relief to Tigger as Aunt Evelyn could be very stern at times and he feared the sharp end of her tongue, but it was not to be and she was nothing but kind and sympathetic. Tigger feared he would be sent straight home, or at least after a day or so, but in the event he was to stay for a while.

After a good night's sleep, Tigger wondered what the new day would bring. It was decided that he would be best off going with Aunts Evelyn and Phyl to the factory in Leicester. Tigger thought this was great. Time spent in the Directors Suite, with grand wooden panelled walls, a large leather surfaced desk and an array of pens, pencils, cabinets with files and drinks. He was given an escorted tour of the factory, which he found most fascinating. All these people working rows and rows of machinery, miles of cotton reels and big containers where materials were dyed in different colours. He had never seen anything like it and Aunt Evelyn owned all this!!!

One day whilst in the Directors Suite Aunt Evelyn thought it was about time Tigger spoke to his father. Tigger felt very nervous about this but knew he had to do it one day. His father was so calm and spoke only about what Tigger had been up to, how did he feel and was he happier? No mention of running away or bad reports, also no mention whether he wanted to speak to his mother. What a relief and a first hurdle negotiated. Tigger felt better after speaking to his father.

One day whilst at the factory, Aunt Phyl got hold of Tigger and said,

"Come on, let's go shopping – you need some new clothes."

Off they went into the city centre and found one of the best clothes shops. Tigger's parents had forwarded a parcel of clothes to his Gran but Aunt Phyl felt it was high time Tigger had some good casual clothes other than school uniform and play clothes.

"Choose anything you want," she said.

Tigger could not believe it. He had never had anyone say this to him before. His mother and father did not have the money available for him to have a free for all. With the guidance of Aunt Phyl Tigger chose an array of clothes. Shirts, trousers, a sports jacket, sweaters and socks, all fitted like a glove. He felt on top of the world and could hardly believe that this was happening. He was no longer a boy but a young man.

As it was Easter the aunts took time away from the factory. Their car was packed and off they all went to Happisbugh and cliff top bungalow.

Tigger loved going to Happisburgh. For Tigger this was heaven. He could not have been further away from his troubles down in Sussex. The beach and sea was endless and there were children in many of the other holiday bungalows along the cliff top. He soon made friends and days were spent playing on the beach, free from any nagging and shouting. There were also old war emplacements where guns used to be and underground bunkers where ammunition may have been stored. Pitch black it was, frightening but oh so much fun.

Some days the aunts and Tigger would be off to a local farm to pick fresh strawberries in the fields, which Tigger had never done before. Other days were spent on the Norfolk Broads on a motor boat. He felt so privileged and yet it was the normal thing to do. He wished the holiday could last forever. But it was not to be and soon they were on the journey back to Swithland in Leicestershire and to Gran. It was also time to think about going back home to Sussex and to Mum and Dad, something Tigger knew was inevitable but also something he was dreading. Tigger's bicycle would go back separately from him but he would go back by train. The farmer, Mr Walker, next door to Grans, wryly enquired,

"Are they going to make you cycle back down to Sussex then, Lad?"

Gran was sad to see Tigger go and hoped all would be well on his return home, as he closed the car door and they made the journey to Leicester Central Station. Both the aunts were full of advice and assurances that things would be better back home in Sussex, but Tigger was not so sure. A horrible feeling was coming over him as he kissed them both farewell as he boarded the steam train to London and on then on to Sussex. He felt that the good times were over once more.

On the way down to London on the train a man started talking to Tigger. He felt uneasy about this man and tried to ignore him. He invited Tigger down to the Pullman car where he bought Tigger some refreshments. Tigger was becoming more and more uneasy about this man. On the way back to their compartment the man tried to pull Tigger into a toilet, telling it would be OK, he would not harm him. Somehow Tigger managed to pull free and get back to his seat with other people. The man did not speak to Tigger until they arrived at London. When they were walking up the platform the man tried to touch Tigger and then ran off into the crowd. The journey back was going to be bad enough without this happening and Tigger was too scared to say anything and never told anyone about this the rest of his life. A taxi across London to Victoria and onto the train to Angmering felt like the longest journey of Tigger's life. The walk from the station to home was one of the worst walks he had encountered. Would his mother have had to mull things over during his stay up in Leicestershire? Would she show any compassion? Would she even feel any guilt over the way she had treated Tigger? The click of the gate and up to the back door, how would Mum react? He passed the kitchen window and his heart sank as he saw her expression as their eyes met through the window.

"Oh, you have decided to come home at last then?"

That said it all!

It was late afternoon and would only mean Tigger had to endure a couple of hours before his father was home. In the meanwhile his mother lectured him on how he should be ashamed of himself causing so much trouble. She also commented that she was told not to say too much to him for fear of bringing on one of her asthma attacks! Tigger took that with a pinch of salt.

At last Tigger's Dad arrived home, and much to his relief his Dad was so pleased to see him and gave him a hug and a kiss – something that was rare for him to do and something his mother definitely had not done.

The evening passed more pleasantly than Tigger had envisaged. Questions were asked about Tigger's cycle journey up to Leicester. Had he not wished or thought about turning back, had he slept on the way and if so, where? Uncle Mike had commented to his parents that Tigger must have been very fit to have arrived in Leicester so quickly.

"He must have a very sound heart!"

A typical Uncle Mike comment.

It was much to Tigger's relief that there were only two more days before he returned to school. During those two days, holiday homework had to be done, odd jobs around the garden and endure the odd atmosphere. He also had to buy a box of chocolates for the local policeman, write a short note of apology and deliver them to his house. To his relief the policeman was out, and so he left them with the policeman's wife.

Chapter 12
The Return
to School

It was obvious to Tigger that many of the school staff would be aware of what had happened during the past few weeks, some of the boys may also have been made aware. News like that gets around fast! He was curious to know what the reaction would be and how he would be treated. Treated with respect, bullied or nothing? Tigger was really quite proud of what he had done, not for the reasons he had to do it but for the sense of achievement. In fact, Tigger would have been quite disappointed if nothing was said at school about his adventure. Well he was not to be disappointed and one of the boys in his class, Brand, a boy who had an air of leadership about him was the first to bring up the subject. He came straight out with it.

"What did you run away for, then, Warri?"

In next to no time a whole crowd of boys was circling Tigger, eager to hear the story of Tigger Running Away! As a grammar school such things were unheard of so Tigger had caused quite a stir – he was not exactly one of the 'in crowd' – not a boarder so for the rather timid Tigger had done something that made many of them sit up and take note! Tigger did not go into any great detail about the reasons leading up to his running away, but most of the boys were very sympathetic to his plight.

It was Brand, yet again, who brought Tigger back down to earth, a bit, with his passing comment.

"Well that will teach you a thing or two for mucking about in class!"

I suppose he was right in some respects, but none of them knew how home life had been so terrible.

One or two of the masters commented to Tigger about his adventure and the games master remarked that he would now expect great results from Tigger in Cross Country and Athletics.

February x-country and into the freezing cold water

In the end not a lot else was said. Tigger was relieved as he did not want to continually be the centre of attention. He did confide in Johnny and Piers about what happened and he knew they both thought his mother was rather an odd bod! Mr Curtis, his maths teacher, with whom he had bonded with well, had remarked that it was no more than he had expected. Mr Curtis, a small bespectacled man had rather taken Tigger under his wing, as it were. He had picked up body language and vibes that Tigger was not a happy boy. He had suggested after school maths tuition. The school owned an old large house across the road from the main school, Westover. It was here that some of the school masters lived and it was also where the school 6th form was located. In the basement was the school Cadet Force Stores. It was in Westover where Tigger was to have his extra tuition and where Mr Curtis was to get to know Tigger a lot better.

Tigger enjoyed the company of Mr Curtis and the way he taught maths. He made it more interesting. He was known to all at school as Tricky Curtis. When teaching in the classroom he would very often say that a particular maths problem was 'Very Tricky' so he became Tricky Curtis. Many of the masters had nick names given to them by the boys that became permanent throughout the life of the school. Tricky Curtis became a friend and they often had tea before the extra lessons, and they talked about many different subjects, hobbies, likes and dislikes. Tricky appreciated Tigger's problems at home and promised to help whenever he could. He was a good Christian man with no hidden agenda. He wanted to get to know Tigger's mother so he could try and work out what the problems were and to this end, on

82

occasions, Tricky and Tigger would have the tea and extra maths lessons at Tigger's home. Tricky would take Tigger back home in his car. Tigger recalls that on one occasion his mother was ranting how Tigger was useless, he had a brain but was too lazy to use it, he will never achieve anything in life unless he pulls his socks up she would say.

Tricky tried to reason with her by saying Tigger needed encouragement not being constantly told how useless he was and no good at anything. That did not go down at all well. Tricky also said he believed part of the problem was that Tigger was afraid of his mother.

"You're not afraid of me, are you?"

"No, Mum."

"See, he's not afraid of me. What a load of nonsense, how dare you suggest such a thing!"

But Tricky was no fool and he could see through it all. Unfortunately there was little he could do, other than give Tigger support whenever he could. He was sympathetic and he would advise Tigger whenever possible. Home life really had not improved at all since Tigger had returned from his stay with his grandmother at Swithland and he was getting more and more depressed about life. His school work continued to suffer. He liked certain subjects, such as, geography, English and history, but chemistry, physics and maths he could not make any headway. School reports continued to be poor. There was another school trip abroad to Denmark, but he did not even bother to tell his parents, it was pointless as he knew there was no chance of him being able to go. It made him feel very low as all the other boys were going to go, even John asked if he could have a chat with Tigger's mother to try and persuade her to let Tigger go.

Chapter 13
Life Gets Worse Gran Dies

Unbeknown to Tigger, Gran had not been well for some time. There was no phone at home and therefore any time a call had to be made, Tigger's mum and dad had to either use the local telephone box round the corner or use a neighbours telephone. The doorbell rang one evening and it was one of the neighbours. Mum and Dad were gone some time and Tigger wondered what was going on. Eventually they returned to the lounge, his mother in tears and looking daggers at Tigger.

"Your grandmother has died and you have murdered her!"

Tigger was aghast at what his mother had said.

"She's dead, and all because of you!"

Tigger's father told his mother to calm down and it was not fair to say such a dreadfully wicked thing.

"It's true – if he had not run away and caused me mam to worry so much she would not have got cancer and she would be alive today."

As one can imagine there was a very sombre feeling in the household and Tigger just wanted to go to his room. And those tears his mother shed? *Crocodile tears,* he thought.

It was not long before Tiger, his mum and dad were up in Leicester for the funeral. It was the first time Tigger had been to a funeral and it soon became all too much for him, breaking down as the reality hit home that he would never see his lovely grandmother again. No more holidays spent enjoying himself at Swithland. He also thought how futile and hypocritical it all was. Everyone seemingly enjoying themselves tucking into food after the funeral, chatting away and then talk of who was having what pieces of furniture and what was to become of Gran's house.

Well it was soon all over. Mum had to stay on in Swithland to sort out Gran's house, paperwork and all that sort of stuff that goes on after someone dies. To Tigger it was a relief as he and his dad would be on their own for a while without the nagging and moaning from his mother. Before the funeral, Tigger had been given a note to take to school saying he would be off school for a while because of the funeral. The note from his father did not say how long Tigger would be off school.

Once at home it seemed pleasantly quiet, just Dad and Tigger. Quite a peaceful atmosphere. But Tigger could not get out of his head that he would never see his gran again. He wanted time on his own. So, on a whim, he decided he would not go back to school when his Dad returned to work. He spent the days either staying at home lazing around whilst his Dad was at work, going to Brighton ice skating, which he loved or going to the cinema. The school would not be in touch as they had had a note to say Tigger would not be at school.

After about a week to ten days, she – his mother was back. All doom and gloom.

Tigger went back to school and no one was the wiser – for now!

At the end of term all was revealed. The school report had an attendance record. As well as noting the additional days absent, the school master also noted that it was a shame Tigger had to miss almost two weeks schooling because of the funeral, which was probably a contributory factor to poor results that term! The reaction at home was quite predictable. Tigger's father was sad more than angry and Tigger sensed he understood. His mother, however, subjected Tigger to more abuse.

"Whilst I was laying to rest a poor old lady, driven to her grave by you, you were out enjoying yourself with no regard or thought for your dead grandmother lying cold in her grave or me, and whilst your father was out working hard to earn money to pay for your private education. You should be thoroughly ashamed of yourself."

Tigger had just wanted to get away from everything for a while, a bit of freedom.

The holiday was no holiday, Tigger either had to work the whole time at home doing jobs around the house or garden and in between do a holiday job at the local nursery. There was no time spent with friends. Tiger was ashamed to bring friends to his home as his mother was so embarrassing. Most of them thought she was an oddball and Tigger was envious of his friends' mothers as they all seemed to be such loving and kind people. He loved going to his friends home.

After a while things settled down at home and things improved slightly. Tigger believed that his father had some words with his mother and the moaning and abuse seemed to abate somewhat. Tigger had made his mind up to try harder at school and concentrate on his studies – difficult as that was going to be.

Tigger has always been in the A stream at school, but the school had been in touch with his parents. It was felt that Tigger could benefit from being dropped into the B stream in order for him to catch up with some of his studies that he had dropped behind in. Tigger was unaware of this. No one had told him! So it was a great shock and shame for him, returning to school after the holidays, to read the form lists in the main hall that he was dropped to Lower VB instead of Lower VA.

There was almost a 'Class' distinction between the A and B streams. There he was in a class with students who were unfamiliar to him. To him it was humiliating.

One particular student – Monger – was intent on humiliating Tigger even more by picking on him and goading him on.

"How does it feel to be dropped into the B Stream, Warrington? Ha ha."

"Got no friends in here, have you?"

Mr Petherbridge, the form master was unaware of the impending fracas as he was busy completing first day paper formalities. Tigger had NEVER been involved in any form of fight or violence at school until now. Monger continued with his goading until Tigger snapped and there was one almighty punch up – punches thrown thick and fast until Tigger picked up a desk, in his pent up furry and launched it at Monger. This sparked Mr Petherbridge into action, helped by other boys in the class and the fight stopped as quickly as it had begun. Both Monger and Tigger had severe bruising about their faces. Tigger a split lip and lots of blood, Monger a large egg sized swelling above an eye.

A rapid visit to the heads office. A threat of expulsion if there was ever a repeat performance, plus six of the best for both of them with the heads SPECIAL cane. Yes it really hurt. In those days corporal punishment was the norm and accepted.

Strange as it may seem both Tigger and Monger became good friends after that episode. Respect, I guess? The wimp from the A Stream could fight back. In those days corporal punishment was the normal way to punish the lads. Cane from the head. Slipper from the maths/PE teacher, the notorious blackboard rubber (solid wood back) used to come flying across the classroom from the English teacher – hurt if it hit your head. Even a twisting of the ear from the French teacher. Everyone accepted it as part and parcel of school life and one dared to not go home to tell their parents for fear of an additional swipe!

Life at school did improve. Tigger was always able to meet up with his pals during break times and the boys in his new class were also OK. Tigger had also joined the school Army Cadet Force. He did not discuss it with his parents. One day one of the senior cadets was on a recruitment drive, came into one of Tigger's classes and that was it. His real father was in the Army! He enjoyed his time on the Thursday afternoon Training Sessions. After an initial training period and learning the basics, he was soon promoted to Lance Corporal and then full Corporal. He liked the discipline, learning new life skills, map reading, shooting, Army Drill and keeping his uniform in top condition – religiously polishing his brasses and boots. Occasionally weekend manoeuvres would be arranged by the CO-Commanding Officer, the school history master, Mr Bacon, with the local Territorial Army Unit at Southwick, which the lads enjoyed trying to beat them every time. Tigger so enjoyed this part of his school life that, at one time he seriously considered an Army career. At that time he had no idea his birth father was also a Career Soldier in the Royal Army Medical Corp. Something he was to discover many years later. His mother had said they would try and get him into the Pay Corp as he would not get enough qualifications for anything better. As it happened no further progress was made to pursue that career!

During Tigger's first few months in the Cadets he had found great comradery and his good friend Johnny Scadgel had also joined the Force which pleased him immensely. The school had its own small rifle range behind the school chapel and its own armoury within the school. Tigger was eventually trusted with being in charge of the armoury and the keys. It was amazing in those days that a school entrusted a young lad with such responsibility. The armoury contained a variety of weapons. .22 Rifles, Lee Enfield .303 Rifles, Sten guns and Bren Guns – all in full working order. Also dummy hand grenades and ammunition. Occasionally Tigger and a couple of others would smuggle a couple of .22 Rifles and go across the road to the school range and have a practice and also at the local church weathervane high up on the church tower! Taking great delight at seeing it spin round rapidly when their shots were on target. Expulsion came to mind had they ever been caught!

Apart from term time training and the odd weekend the Cadet Force always went to a summer Army Camp. Tigger's first one was maybe the most memorable. It was at Borley Camp at Aldershot, Four thousand cadets under canvas, quite an experience. Training was mostly desert warfare and regular Army tank and artillery demonstrations. The local soil was very sandy so ideal for that kind of training. The highlight of the week was Sunday Church Parade. To hear four thousand cadets marching along the road to the arena was something to behold. Unbeknown to all, that great soldier taking the march past salute was none other than Field Marshal Bernard Montgomery. A very proud and moving occasion for all the boys. After the parade many of the boys' parents came up to see them and to his surprise Tigger's parents came too! He was quite moved and surprised, and proud to show off his uniform and the quarters where he was billeted. Tents with straw filled mattresses!

It was soon back to school and to his delight the one term in the B Stream had the desired effect and he was back in the A Stream, and back with his friends – Johnny, Piers, Tony Michael Roger and a few others. Time was rapidly approaching for the GCE Exams, so Tigger was determined to do his best in everything at school including sport. He loved his sport as he was so competitive. It gave him an opportunity to shine away from home and away from his mother. He was never happier than when he was running over the South Downs on the Cross Country Run. He felt so free, able to run and run. He liked football but he was in his element at Cross Country. He was also good at it but could never manage to beat one of the other lads – Pellatt. He was a good runner and put plenty of hours training in going up and down the shingle on the beach. Tigger was always second best to Pellatt – no matter how hard he tried. The following summer on the run up to the Annual Sports Day Tigger and Pellatt did a lot of training for the Mile, the most prestigious race and carried a lot of points towards the Victor Ludorum Cup for the best all round performance. Tigger also trained for the 880 yards and the long jump. He was also first reserve for the 440 yards.

Come the day many of Tigger's friends had their parents supporting their sons. Tigger's father always worked on a Saturday so could not be there, however his mother was able to go but was never there to give Tigger support and encouragement. He felt sad but also determined to do his best in his events. On the day he had only been entered into the Mile and first reserve for the 440 yards. The Mile was his target and he took no notice of the 440 yards as he would not be running in that anyway – so he thought!

After chatting to his friends and doing some warm ups he suddenly noticed that he had not seen Pellatt.

"Has anyone seen Pellatt? Has anyone seen Pellatt?"

No one had seen him. Tigger asked one of the sports masters,

"Have you seen Pellatt, Sir?"

"No, we gather he is not coming, not well or something."

Wow! NOT COMING!!! Now was his one chance at the end of his school career to win the MILE!!! He was so wrapped up in the euphoria that he almost missed a call over the PA system.

"Warrington, call for Warrington for the 440yards."

Heck what was going on? Tigger rushed across to ask,

"What's going on? I am only first reserve and I am entered in the Mile shortly after?"

"Can't help that, Warrington, David Titcomb has not turned up and you are first reserve. Now get ready."

The 440 was by no means his best event, his forte was the longer runs. He did his best but came in 4th or 5th and pretty shattered!!! Two or three events after was the MILE!!! They were off and Tigger was away hoping to create some distance between himself and the other runners, but after about three and a half laps his legs began to feel like lead and he could hear the panting of another runner rapidly approaching him and then overtake him. Talmey!!! What the heck was he doing overtaking him? Needless to say, Talmey won and Tigger was second. The lovely cup had been snatched from his grasp! He was gutted. Also the chance of winning the Victor Ludorum. The irony was that ten days later Tigger was to beat Talmy in the Sussex School Mile by around 30 seconds. Small consolation. You win some, you lose some!

At the end of term was Tigger's second Army Cadet Camp at St Martins Plain Folkestone. Not a bad camp and as usual a good time was had by all, but not as good a camp as Aldershot.

Chapter 14
Final Year at School
GCE Results

At the first school assembly the GCE results were read out for all to hear. Tigger's friends had passed two or three and he wondered why his name had not been called out?

"Why has my name not been called out when you read out the GCE results, Sir?"

"That's because you did not pass any, Warrington!"

What none, he thought. He was numb with shock and shame – and fear of what the reaction would be at home.

Going home slowly he could not imagine what was going to be said or how his mother would react – the ground could have swallowed him up. As one can imagine there was much moaning and groaning and throwing back at him how much money they had spent on his education, the sacrifices they had made and what a waste of space he was. How he would end up on the streets – a tramp, just like his mother!

Having got over the initial trauma and shock of being a failure, the constant nagging from his mother, the gradual wearing down of confidence, Tigger was determined to be the worm that turned and show what he could do! With a new resolve he returned to the final year of school with a determination to try and succeed at both sport and his studies.

He was to get the support of some of his teachers, his friends and his sports masters. Little, if anything was known or spoken about dyslexia in those days, but subsequently Tigger believed he was dyslexic – maybe as a result of his mother changing him from left to right handed – it may have confused his brain!

His studies improved to a reasonable standard. Cross country was again very competitive but he just could not beat Pelatt, but Tigger always came a very good second but was always first on those occasions Pelatt was not there. The school entered a team for the Sussex School Cross Country Championships at Stanmer Park by Sussex University. A large number were entered, around 400 boys over a five or six mile course. The school team started well and soon Tigger and Pelatt were pulling away and up with the front runners. Then bad luck was to strike Tigger yet again. A runner suddenly overtook striking his spiked shoe on Tigger knee. It was quite painful and bled somewhat, then in an attempt to run through the pain the stitch struck, for the first time that season. Digging his fingers deep into his lower ribs he attempted to rid himself of the pain. Runners were passing Tigger in great numbers whilst he stumbled along attempting to keep going. Eventually the pain went and he was again on his way, feeling good and striding past runners. No way would he be able to make up places to compete with the top few, but to do well was his aim. Eventually with the finishing line crossed he had come around 52nd. Not bad out of over 400 and with the two injuries. Pelatt had done well finishing 4th. If only he had not been held back he too may have been nearer Pelatt. He went on to represent the school at the All England Cross Country Championship near Liverpool and came within the first 30. A commendable result.

The school year seemed to pass quickly and it was soon GCE Exam time again and Tigger felt more confident of passing some subjects this time around. The end of term and the year was rapidly approaching and it would all be over. All these years at Shoreham Grammar, a good school with good friends and school masters who gave Tigger a lot of support through difficult times. It was going to be sad. Then it was there, the final day. Farewells were said, promises to meet up etc. But for some it was not quite the end. There was cadet camp. Summer Cadet Camp that final year was at Thetford Army Camp. The day after the end of term those going to Camp returned to school to load up the coach with all the equipment needed for ten days camp including all the rifles. It was a long journey with a lot of banter and baudy Army songs! It was an excellent and large camp. Tigger was promoted to sergeant and very proud he was to finish his Cadet career with a promotion. The time at that camp was truly exciting, good friends having a good time and soon they were all on the long return coach journey back to an empty school. That was really the end of school! Promises to keep in touch with one another and then emotional farewells.

Time soon passed and the brown envelope popped through the door to announce Tigger's results. Three passes and three near passes. Again better but not good enough! It was never good enough.

"Well, you will never get a decent job with just THREE 'O-Levels' – we will have to see what can be done!" said his mother.

An application for a place at Worthing College of Further Education was made together with a grant. After a successful interview, a place was offered for an 'O-Level' course with the option for a further year for an advanced course.

Tigger was looking forward to this new phase in his education. It was not school, some of his schoolmates would also be there, there was no school uniform and lessons may actually be interesting. The other thing? There would be GIRLS at the college as well.

On enrolment day everyone introduced each other. A mixed, but pleasant bunch of guys n gals. Introductions were made to the course tutor – yes, TUTOR not TEACHER. Although it was only his first day, Tigger immediately began to feel at ease and felt he was going to enjoy this college life – and so it was to be. It was strange as Tigger found that there were more students that he knew at the college than he had anticipated. They were all treated as adults and not as pupils. There was little or no discipline as none seemed to be required. There was obviously a lot of banter but no unruly behaviour.

All the tutors, without exception, had a way of teaching that made all the subjects interesting – even maths! Now maths was Tigger's nightmare and he never felt confident enough to contemplate even managing to pass his exams. HOWEVER, here at college was Miss Wright and she certainly was Miss RIGHT! She was a real cracker and all the lads wanted Miss Wright to give them extra help! Seriously – she was a lovely person, maybe not long out of college/university herself and she made even maths interesting. It was bad enough trying to understand Algebra, Geometry and Trigonometry BUT the course even included

CALCULUS!!! What the heck was that? But Miss Wright to the rescue and explained there could only be SIX questions to choose from and as long as the students learned them off by heart, there would be no problem. Simple!!!

Soon all the students were getting on well with one another and often socialised outside college. They had their own common room and managed to get furniture, a record player, records and a table tennis table, all on a very small budget. They even had their own fire in the winter. Good friends were made and in particular Dave, a lad who lived in nearby Rustington.

Tigger was, at last, beginning to really enjoy life, his confidence was building and girls were starting to fancy him, but that is one area that he lacked confidence! He could chat away to them but as far as a date? He was far too shy, he was scared of rejection. Tigger enjoyed his studies and as a result his reports were good. Home life started to improve and his mother began to mellow somewhat.

It was the end of the first term and Christmas was just around the corner. Christmas was always traditional, sometimes Grandmother would come down from Swithland, but this Christmas it was just the three of them. The usual turkey and trimmings for lunch – to be on the table by 1 o'clock so washing up could be done and sat down in the lounge ready for the Queen's speech, to which Mother always stood up for the National Anthem!

Christmas Day was good until Boxing Day arrived.

Chapter 15
Dad Falls Ill

Dad had been drinking a lot on Christmas Day – neither of them ever drank alcohol – so it was juices. It was put down to the rich food. This continued on Boxing Day, which gave cause for some concern. Suddenly Dad passed out. Although Boxing Day, the doctor arrived in no time at all and after some injections Dad seemed to recover quite quickly. Diabetes was diagnosed and after a number of telephone calls the doctor asked if Dad could get up to Guys Hospital in London. Trains were running so Tigger volunteered to accompany him. Having stabilised him and passed fit to travel, they set off to London.

It had started to snow on the journey up to London and by the time they arrived there was quite a covering. Snow had been forecast so it was no surprise. A taxi to Guys in a blizzard. They stopped at the gates to the hospital but slid right past in the very icy conditions!

Having got his Dad bedded in and comfortable as far as one can be in hospital, Tigger had to find his way back to Victoria Station. Tigger thought he would save the taxi fare by taking the Circle line back to Victoria, only to find, after about four stations, that he was going the wrong way around the Circle Line!

He was soon on the train back to Angmering Station and home, by midnight.

Mum and Tigger were very worried about Dad and kept in touch with Guys to check on his progress. Mum became so agitated one evening at dinner time that she let fly at Tigger by slashing him across the hand with a knife – fortunately the knife was not that sharp, but still drew blood. Tigger had dinner by himself – he was beginning to stand up for himself.

Dad was soon stabilised in hospital and home. Insulin injections twice a day for the rest of his life. Careful monitoring of his food, particularly sugar content. Food was weighed daily until he was used to his new diet. It became part of his life and apart from a few 'hypo' attacks life soon reverted back to normality.

Chapter 16
Tigger's First Holiday
Away From Parents

College days were to continue to be very happy. Further friendships were made and Tigger joined the local Young Conservatives and made further friends – a move that was to reap rewards later in life!

Tigger's studies continued to be interesting, results were good, students got up to all kinds of harmless pranks. Tigger had already made up his mind to stay on at college for a further year to enrol for either an A-Level Course or business studies. The summer was very hot and although studies were attended, on occasions it was better fun to skip some afternoon classes and either go down to the beach or play tennis on the College Courts. Tigger and a group of his friends decided to book a two week holiday to Spain – through the College, who were able to negotiate discounts – to Lloret de Mar on the Costa Brava. Including all the travel costs – 35 pounds!!! Before that were exams, but Tigger felt so much more confident than when he had been at school, even maths was not too bad! Exams over and it was off to sunny Spain.

Tigger and his friends – including Dave – really enjoyed the journey. A cross channel ferry to France and a train to Paris, across Paris to Paris Austerlitz Station and on the overnight Barcelona Express. A terrific journey highlighted by a morning sunrise over the sea near Perpignan. They were met by a taxi at a remote station up in the hills and then it was down to Lloret and the hotel. Two weeks away with your mates and no parents, what could be better? No restrictions on alcohol or what time to get in at night. FREEDOM!!! Tans were already good from the good start to the English summer – a good tan was a must and GIRLS!!! Long days on the beach, a visit to Barcelona and a bull fight – never again! And loads of long boozy nights joining in the flamenco and street dancing.

Once home from the holiday life seemed to get a little better. Tigger was gaining in confidence, getting more independent, going out with friends, just how life should be for a growing young man. Soon exam results arrived and for Tigger, he was pleased with his four passes. He had done what he set out to do and it was a basis for a way forward. To Tigger's mother – the passes were OK but not good enough grades. Tigger really couldn't care less what she thought – and Tigger's Dad? He was kind and pleased. That made Tigger feel good.

Tigger returned to College having enrolled in a Chartered Institute of Secretary Business Studies Course. He loved the course – with the exception of accounts. The course tutor was a Mr Illius, an ex-company accountant. Immaculately presented in expensive suits, a typical English upper class accent with a lisp, Tigger just could not get to grips with company accounts. He loved Law, Economics and Economic Geography.

Tigger became more involved with College life and was soon voted in as Student Union Chairman. Girls were attracted to Tigger. He became so involved with various activities, including sport, Union Meetings, speaking, that he became quite well known within the College community. Being chairman he also had the keys to the Union office, which was very convenient for PRIVATE meetings with girlfriends!

Worthing was quite a sleepy town, predominantly a retired population. At a meeting of the Union one day, a discussion started about how good it would be to put Worthing ON THE MAP! The College had never had a RAG WEEK. But the consensus was to organise something that would be sensational? How about dressing up as Robin Hood and his Merry Men and taking over the local Arundel Castle, home to the Duke of Norfolk, the premier Roman Catholic in the UK. How ridiculous – it could never be done and do not include Tigger as he does not like heights!

After many meetings, reconnaissance visits to Arundel, locating the best way to scale the Castle wall and a date to be set for the stunt they were to hold the castle to ransom hoping to get money for a National Cancer Charity.

It was by coincidence the day before the Castle was due to open for the season – at Easter – there was to be an archery contest in the Castle grounds, a good reason for the national press and TV companies to be there. The press and TV companies had been tipped off about the student stunt and would not miss the opportunity to cover such a story.

Come the day, eight students set off for Arundel for their SAS style mission. No one but the EIGHT were privy to what was about to happen. No friends, no parents, no one! Having parked their cars outside of town, the park wall was scaled and the eight set off across the grassy parkland all dressed as various Robin Hood characters – much to the amazement and surprise of many courting couples lying in the grass! Arriving at the Castle wall on the north side of the battlements, it certainly looked a lot more daunting than had been envisaged. First one over secured the grappling iron and rope. Tigger managed to get up with little or no problem. Once all over, they all managed to scale further interior walls until they were standing onhe Keep and one of the guys played *When the Saints*, the call sign for the press and TV cameras to cover the student stunt! After about 20 minutes a loan Arundel policeman arrived to arrest them all. The main gates to the Castle were opened and the students marched out, arms raised to the gathering of the National press and TV cameras. After a warning from the police they were released and they all made their way back home. Tigger's parents had no idea what had been happening, only that a group of friends were going for a walk in Arundel Park – what a nice thing for a group of friends to do they thought!!!

Tigger's mother ALWAYS watched the ten o'clock News on TV.

"Oh look – there's something about Arundel Castle!"

Suddenly the penny dropped!

"SO, that's what you were up to this afternoon? What a disgrace, what will the neighbours say?"

Blah Blah.

The daily newspapers arrived the next day. Worthing certainly was put on the map!

Headlines with FULL page photos in many of the tabloids, names, addresses.

On their return to college everyone was full of it. All the talk was about the stunt. They were all hauled up before the principle and they feared a rollicking. The office door was closed behind them and the principal, Mr Mason, looked them up and down as he sat behind his desk.

"What were you lot up to yesterday? BLOODY well done!!! You have certainly put Worthing and the College on the map."

After handshakes all round, they were all sworn to secrecy as to what Mr Mason had said – and CERTAINLY no word to the press, who were dying for an interview from the Famous Eight.

Tigger felt his dad was silently proud that his son had been part of such a daring stunt, but dared not say anything for fear of what his mum would say. Gradually the moaning about it all died down and life returned to normal. The Eight achieved a lot of kudos – particularly with the girls. What a change life at Worthing College had given Tigger. Confident, friendships, leadership, achievement – still not that confident with relationships with the girls on a one to one basis but he was so much happier with his life, which was so important to him. He so wanted a girlfriend, someone to love outside of the family circle. He went out with one or two girls after pressure to do so from THEIR friends but usually only on a one night stand. His relationship with his mother had improved, but it was by no means perfect and there was always that haunting doubt that things could fall apart. Although he had good friends and went out socially Tigger was still expected to do jobs around the house and help in the garden and sometimes had to put off a social event as he felt obliged to be on hand to do a job or two. His father did not enjoy the best of health so was happy to help him on occasions. Tigger always kept in touch with Aunt Peta to let her know how things were and what he was up to.

Tigger completed his second year course at College – Institute of Secretary Business Studies. He sat the five exams and came out with good results. He remained good friends with Dave and they continued to socialise after their college days.

Chapter 17
Tigger's First Job

School and college were behind him and Tigger had to find a job – a career. Uncle Mike was very helpful in advising Tigger what his options could be. He could find Tigger a job in the city but as he said,

"I feel it would be of more benefit to you if you found your own job, and went through the process yourself – I can offer you advice if you need any."

A few applications were made, one of which was to the Westminster Bank and soon an invite to an interview was received in London at their head office.

A smart suit was purchased at the local tailor, Burtons and come the day of the interview Tigger made his way to London and Westminster Bank head office on his own. Quite a daunting experience for a young man setting out on his career path, but nevertheless he made a good account of himself and as is usual in such cases, he was told, they would let him know in due course.

Although confident, Tigger was a little apprehensive about the outcome and thought it could go either way.

The postman arrived with a letter and stamped on the envelope was Westminster Bank. With butterflies in his stomach he tore open the envelope and the first line of the letter told him it was positive!

'We are pleased to able to offer... etc etc.'

His mother was pleased with the outcome and told Tigger not to mess up this opportunity of a good professional career – always a negative side. Tigger could not wait for his father to come home so he could get REAL and genuine praise.

The letter offered Tigger a place at the local Westminster Branch in Rustington. All he had to do was to acknowledge the letter and accept the position, which he did without delay.

He was to report to the branch manager, Mr Hicks at 9 a.m. What could be better than a job at the local branch? So on Monday morning, off on his bicycle to Rustington his mother and father wished him luck.

Mr Hicks, the manager, was a tall, bald headed man, well-spoken and friendly. Introductions were duly made to the other members of staff, seven in all, and Tigger, being the junior member, had typical tasks to do for a job of that type in those days.

"Can you make a good cup of tea, Warrington?" Mr Hicks asked.

"Yes, Sir."

"Good, that's your first job in the morning and then Caroline will show you the job you will be learning."

They were a good bunch of people. Mr Wilson was the first clerk/deputy manager who was a slightly odd character who seemed to lack total confidence although good at his job, he seemingly would never have a branch of his own. He lived locally and cycled to and from the branch each day, cycle clips firmly around his trouser bottoms. During even the hot weather the men were never allowed to take their jackets off and Wilson used to sweat profusely, so much so that his body salt used to form in rings under his jacket armpits. Something the girls in the office used to point at as they passed behind him!

After a short time Tigger was sent on the bank's month initial training course as Oaken Holt in Oxfordshire, a grand old house owned by the bank. There were about 30 on the course from branches all around the country. It was a good month and the middle weekend students were allowed home – and his then girlfriend, Erika; yes, he had at last got himself a very good looking girlfriend – had gone off with another chap, much to Tigger's disgust and disappointment. He could not wait to get back to Oaken Holt where HE had already got his eye on an attractive young lady from Oldham – Chrissy. A romance started in between lessons! The course was soon over, necessary tests and exams passed and Tigger was back at his branch.

Tigger soon progressed in the job and gained confidence with the tasks given him. In those days there were no computers so all bank statements were typed out on an accounting machine – which Tigger was very proficient with, four sets of ledgers covering the alphabet were completed daily by hand, cheques and credits were entered and had to be balanced with the sheets from the accounting machine. Banking in the old days!!!

At the end of Tigger's first year, Mr Hicks called him into his office.

"Close the door behind you, Warrington."

Goodness what was this all about, thought Tigger.

"Well this is the end of your first year here. How are you enjoying your time?"

"Yes, Sir, I am enjoying my time very much, thank you."

"Well, we are happy with you and I have completed your first report and as a result, I have had a notification from head office in which the bank has awarded you your first merit award of fifty pounds a year, which will be added to your salary – well done, lad."

Tigger went back out into the office beaming from ear to ear. The rest of the staff were full of congratulations. He went home that evening feeling very good about himself and his parents were also full of praise.

Chapter 18
Life Outside Work

Whilst Tigger was enjoying himself at work his social life also blossomed. As said before, he was a member of the Young Conservatives, which in truth was not very political, but more a social club. It was local so he could always ride down on his bike on Monday evenings. The hall had a badminton court and facilities for refreshments. There were a very mixed bunch and all of them got on well together. Romances soon blossomed with some of them.

Tigger soon became nominated as group chairman, taking over from Derek Whitaker – someone who would have a great influence on his life some years later and with a good committee, he started to arrange an interesting programme of events with speakers covering a variety of topics. It was a time during the Cold War and at one committee meeting it was discussed whether a member of the Russian Embassy could be invited and persuaded to give the membership a talk. Imagine, the Russians talking to the Conservatives. What a coup that would be. An invitation was sent to the Russian Embassy in London. Not really expecting to get a response, let alone a positive one, it was with enormous surprise and elation that the Embassy replied saying they would welcome the opportunity to send one of the Embassy staff to give a talk.

The evening arrived and to a packed hall with many having to stand. The Russian who gave the talk was very friendly but obviously guarded as to how his replies to questions were positioned. The press were in attendance and a good report was made in the local rag.

Good brownie points for Tigger and his committee, it created quite a talking point in the local community for some time. Most of the group in the Conservatives socialised outside the club and everyone seemed to get on so well, parties, meeting at a pub for lunch or in the evening – it really was a good time to be alive. Music in the 60s was also good with The Beatles and many other groups emerging.

Apart from his friends and activities with the Conservative Club Tigger remained friends with some of his pals from his days at Worthing College. A group of them used to spend days out, maybe going to stock car racing or Goodwood Race track, as they had various car race meetings throughout the season, in those days. A couple of his friends by now had their own cars, so they were able to get to various places of interest. Stirling Moss had his notorious crash at Goodwood, which was quite horrific. During Tigger's time at the bank he was able to save a regular amount of money, he was saving for a car. That would certainly improve his social life and not have to be dependent on some of his friends who already had cars. Of course he had to learn to drive first and his dad had a lovely Rover Sports Saloon, a large car, which was not ideal in which to learn to drive. However he coped well and soon passed his test after the third attempt!!! His dad was there to advise him what sort of car would be ideal for his first car.

"A nice little Morris would be ideal – I have seen one on Hares Garage forecourt opposite your bank."

Tigger was not impressed, as he did not like the shape – a bit too old fashioned for his liking, he much preferred the green Ford Consul with a bench front seat and column gear change. It also had a set of those modern indicator lights on the wings, not those silly little yellow wings that flicked out from above the doors!

Tigger won the day, much to the disgust of his mother.

"Why could you not have taken the advice of your dad? Why do you want a big car like that? Blah Blah!!! Big car??? Not that big!"

Tigger loved his car and polished it and it was gleaming, until it looked like new. His mates liked it as more of them could get in it than if Tigger had bought the Morris. On one occasion after his night school classes, he was taking a course for his banking exams he and seven others piled into the car and went to King Alfred Bowl. EIGHT in the car. Four in the front and four in the back. At 3 a.m. after bowling and a bite to eat, they were on their way home when they were stopped by the police. That was it they all thought, overloaded and a fine??? No, police were just checking them out as there had been a local robbery of cash from local phone boxes. The police wished them well and off they went back home. Great times were had in that car.

On many occasions after night school on a Thursday evening Tigger and his friends would rush down into Worthing Town centre to either the Pier Pavilion or the Worthing Assembly Rooms where the up and coming music groups would be playing. They saw many of the groups that went on to make it BIG – The Who, The Kinks, Them Unit 4 Plus 2, The Searches and The Rolling Stones were even there but the lads were too late to get in to see them.

One of his friends, Dave, had a girlfriend from his college days who worked in one of the Worthing banks. She had a friend who she thought would make a good foursome for a date with Tigger. The four of them would go to the cinema and then to a pub afterwards.

A blind date made Tigger feel quite nervous, but he was up for it. They drew up outside the girl's house and Tigger was told to go and knock on the door. THE most gorgeous girl came to the door and Tigger's jaw almost dropped.

"Hello, I am Susan, you must be Tigger?"

"Yes I am. Hello, Susan."

That was the start of a wonderful romance.

Tigger was swept off his feet with Susan. She was a very good looking girl and Tigger was amazed that someone as good looking as her would want to go out with him. It did his confidence the world of good. His mother was also pleased as she came from a good family. Previous girlfriends were 'vetted' and if they lived in a council house they were met with much disapproval! She was the ultimate snob.

Tigger and Susan spent many happy hours at the weekends going to various places, walking on the Downs and having good laughs. She was very spontaneous, always giving Tigger a kiss when they met. Her parents were a joy. Her father was a local solicitor at Malcolm Wilson and Cobby in Worthing. Susan had a younger brother, Michael.

Soon Susan and her friend Victoria joined the Young Conservatives and they blended into Tigger's circle of friends.

Tigger's mother was always moaning about money and even tried to persuade Tigger that when Susan came over for tea at weekends sometimes, that she should get a bus over to save Tigger petrol money. They soon became inseparable, very much in love and Tigger would have done anything for Susan.

It was soon apparent that Tigger's mother was becoming jealous of Susan, saying that they were spending too much time together and Tigger should find other interests. Susan also got on very well with Tigger's father. Both were quite artistic and Susan enjoyed having conversations with him. Tigger's mother had quite limited conversations of interest.

As time went by Tigger was invited to social events at the bank mainly at the Worthing Branch and Susan was invited to these. They were a genuine couple whose social network was growing and Tigger was spending more time with Susan's parents than his own. Tigger's mother was soon finding any excuse to try and keep Tigger at home some weekends with jobs that needed doing because she said his father was unable to do them. But Tigger's father was wise to her tactics and told Tigger not to worry,

"Go and enjoy yourself."

Susan became a little distant from his mother as happened with previous girlfriends and some of his friends. She was an embarrassment, most of Tigger's friends though she was odd. Tigger had never told Susan the full story of how his mother had made his life hell at times and how he had little or no respect for her let alone any love.

114

As time went by and Susan and Tigger's bond became stronger they talked about getting engaged and ultimately, married. Susan agreed that she loved Tigger enough to get engaged and they spoke about how each other's parents would react and how Tigger would approach Susan's parents. Tigger, by this time had a special bond with Susan's parents and felt very easy about approaching the subject of asking their permission to marry Susan – if a little nervous.

The day came when Tigger and Susan, hand in hand, sat in their lounge and Tigger asked Susan's father if he would give permission to marry Susan.

"Of course, Susan's mother and I would be delighted, cannot say we are surprised, we think you are a fine lad and you make a lovely couple, we are very happy."

Susan's mother was in tears with joy and a firm handshake from George, Susan's father.

That weekend Tigger and Susan chose rings for each other, drove up to a quiet spot on the Downs and placed the rings on each other's fingers – they were officially engaged, then back to Susan's house to show off their rings.

Tigger's father was delighted. His mother said she was delighted but Tigger could see her pleasure was slightly muted. Why oh, why could she not let go and be happy for Tigger?

Chapter 19
Things Start To Go Wrong

Tigger and Susan continued to enjoy their romance and the engagement suited them well. Friends were delighted for them. Most of their friends had professional jobs and all seemed to get on well. By this time in the Young Conservatives there were quite a number of couples and some were also engaged.

Work was going well for both of them, Susan worked for the District Bank in Worthing and was a cashier. Tigger was a cashier and safe custody clerk, well-liked by both staff and customers. He had been on further courses and continued with his evening classes for his bankers exams.

Part of his bank training was to get used to how other branches worked and on occasions was seconded to relief staff at one of the banks local branches. This progressed to a full years as relief staff where he worked at a number of different branches all over West Sussex. He enjoyed the experience of not only travelling around but meeting other staff members, doing a variety of jobs. On returning to his home branch in Rustington he was promoted to 1st cashier/securities clerk. He also received an annual merit award subsequent to very good reports from his branch manager, who, by now had changed from Mr Hicks to a Mr Grellier and fine man with a bloody complexion, loved golf and had a rather stern manner about him. Tigger got on well with him and he felt Mr Grellier had a soft spot for him.

On one occasion Tigger was called into his office after an annual report.

"Warrington, I do not know why, but head office seem to think your past years performance deserves another merit award, cannot think why!"

"Well, Mr Grellier, you complete my annual report, so it must have been something you said?"

"Oh, I guess you are right, well congratulations, better get back to the office and carry on your good work."

"Thank you very much, Mr Grellier."

Susan and Tigger continued their happy life. Susan was pleased and proud of Tigger's progress in the bank. It would be a solid start to their married life and they would be able to get a bank loan to buy a house and at staff rates. They talked about getting married and a time scale as to when that may be.

They also talked about going on holiday together for the summer. Susan would love to go to the west country, even as far south as Cornwall. Tigger loved Cornwall as well and had been on a few holidays with his parents to Bude, Polperro and Clovelly. Tigger's Mum and Dad thought it good that they should go on holiday together – just the two of them but why not ask Aunt Evelyn if they could go up to Leicester and then maybe on to Happisburgh to the holiday bungalow on the cliffs. Tigger got in touch with Aunt Evelyn who was more than happy to have them both up there in Swithland or to the Happisburgh bungalow and if they were saving to get married it would save money being spent on a hotel in the west country. Bad move!!! When Tigger approached the subject of the holiday again and mentioned how good it would be to take up Aunt Evelyn's offer, Susan was less than happy. She did not want to spend her holiday with Tigger and two ageing aunts! Anyway, why had Tigger not discussed it with her before going ahead and speaking with his aunts about their holiday?

Tigger had not told Susan that much about his early life and about his mother. So one evening when they were by themselves he started to tell Susan all about his early life and how his mother had treated him and to some degree how she was still trying to control his life. He poured everything out. Susan seemed quite shocked and surprised, but was very sympathetic. Tigger felt she should know and he wanted to get it off his chest.

One day when they had had an evening at Young Conservatives she seemed quite quiet, but said she was OK. Taking her back home that evening she suddenly turned to Tigger and said,

"Never take me for granted, will you?"

"What do you mean by that?"

"Just that, never take me for granted."

Tigger was a little disturbed and felt it an odd thing to say. They continued back to Susan's house in silence. Tigger sensed things were not at all well.

Several weeks passed by after the comment Susan had made. Things between them seemed alright but were they? Tigger asked several times if Susan was OK, was everything between them good? They did not seem to be spending so much time together, Susan wanting to spend time with her girlfriends, which was normal but Tigger just had that uneasy feeling in the back of his mind that something was wrong. The time they spent together was good, but was it as good as it had been?

Tigger was getting more anxious about their relationship and it was playing on his mind. His colleagues at the bank sensed he was not his usual sparky self. Then one day whilst he was on cashier duties he kept giving customers the wrong money. 2, 3, and 4 pounds instead of 20, 30 and 40 pounds. He could not see the nought on the customers cheques. He felt odd in himself, he thought he was going blind. One of the chaps in the office knew there was a problem and took Tigger off the till. He was meeting Susan that evening and he was desperate to let her know he was not well, so his work colleague phoned her bank, spoke to her to let her know Tigger was not well and he would not be meeting her that evening. They took Tigger home and his mother managed to call the doctor. It was his first of many migraine attacks. One evening, after a long day at the bank it was the half year balance when they had to do an audit, he had been out playing squash with a good friend, when suddenly he was talking a load of gibberish, nothing new there then!!! He knew what he wanted to say but the words just would not come out. His cheek felt numb and also his arm. He had to get home quickly before he was unable to drive. He got home and took a pill and went to bed. The next day he felt drained, went to work but had a bad day. It was another migraine manifesting itself in a different way.

Tigger recovered after a day or so but was aware the migraine may have been triggered by his worry over Susan. He knew something was wrong.

He had arranged to meet Susan the following evening at her house. He parked his car and rang the doorbell. George, her father answered the door and Tigger immediately knew all was not well. George's face was not its usual jolly self.

"Come in, Susan has gone out."

They went into the lounge and there were only the two of them.

"As I said, Susan has gone out. There is no easy way of saying this but she cannot face you to tell you, but she cannot carry on. Something is not right with the relationship, she is sorry, she is devastated but cannot face you to tell you and so I said I would have to tell you. It is something to do with your mother and how you told her about your past and how she had treated you. She feels you are still too much under your mother's influence and feels it too big a burden to take on. I really am sorry as we all get on so well together, but if that is how she feels then there is nothing anyone can do about it. I really do not know what to say."

Tigger was dumbfounded. His whole world had totally collapsed. He could not wait to get out of the house. George gave him a hug and told him if at any time he wanted to talk, he would always be there for him. Susan's mother sat in silence with tears rolling down her cheeks. That made Tigger feel worse.

How Tigger managed to get home he will never know. Then he would have to face his parents to tell them.

Chapter 20
A Feeling of Humiliation
and Rejection

Tigger had not had many girlfriends but Susan was someone very special. He blamed himself for how he had acted and not thought of Susan over the holiday episode. Maybe he should not have gone on so much about his mother. A combination of things had obviously left Susan with many doubts as to whether their relationship would last the test of time. Had she met someone else? This had crossed his mind. Tigger's father was very sympathetic and he and Susan had got on very well. His mother although seemingly sorry, did not convey a lot of sorrow or sympathy and was more intent on finding out why Susan had ended the relationship – and anyway she had still got the engagement ring and Tigger needed to get his money back for that, was the main comment. His mother did not tell Tigger that she had been in touch with Susan's parents to arrange a meeting with them and to get the ring back. Tigger was not at all worried about the ring. She sprung it on Tigger one Saturday that they were going to see Susan's parents to 'Have it out with them!' How absolutely humiliating.

It was probably one of the worst times Tigger had experienced. He got on very well with Susan's parents and did not want to put them through his mother's interrogation. The ring was duly handed over and after a very tense meeting, at which Susan's father was most diplomatic and obviously sorry for Tigger, they left the house and Tigger was duly told they were going down into Worthing to the jewellers to get his money back for the ring.

It was, to say the least THE most humiliating and embarrassing day in Tigger's life. A young man of his age should never have his mother ordering him about and trying to take control of things.

"Of course you will never be able to keep a girlfriend – I do not know what's the matter with you – nobody wants you, nobody wanted you when your mother let you go, I was the only one who took you in when no one wanted you!"

He really wanted to tell her to FUCK OFF!

Just what Tigger wanted to hear at a time in his life when he was at his lowest. He felt like a punch bag for all his mother's abuse and nastiness.

Tigger took an age to bring his life back to normal – whatever that was. He had been used to meeting up at weekends with Susan and sometimes during the week, but now his life seemed empty. He stayed in and did not want to meet anyone. He did not even go to Young Conservatives, until one day one of his good friend Mike Shaw came around to see Tigger and gave him a good talking to, pointing out how all the others in The Gang were missing him, that he had to get out and start to rebuild his life. It was a very kind thing to do which Tigger appreciated. Reluctantly Tigger summoned up the energy to go down to Young Conservatives which perked him up somewhat as they were a good crowd and were so pleased to see him. Apparently his good friend Mike had been nominated by the rest of them to speak to Tigger to get him out again. Many of them knew what his mother was like and could not bear the thought of Tigger being cooped up in the bungalow with her.

Gradually he got some of his spark back and started going out again and tried to enjoy life.

Then one Monday evening at Young Conservatives Susan turned up with her friend – they were both members. It was an embarrassing moment for both of them and tugged at Tigger's heart strings. But he rose above it, they exchanged pleasantries and things calmed down.

Tigger decided that his career was not going to suffer as a result of his heartbreak, and so he threw himself into his work, determined to do well. He had a further period of secondment to relief duties of about a year and was promoted yet again with a further merit award. He had been at the Rustington Branch for a few years and he thought that soon a branch move would be on the cards. But not yet.

Now Tigger was not going on holiday with Susan and with his annual leave fast approaching he had to think of something to do during his two week holiday. On a whim he decided he would book up a week at Butlins Holiday Camp at Minehead. It would give him a chance to get away and clear his head. Obviously he knew not a soul when he arrived, having driven down there in his lovely Ford Consul. He soon met up with a couple of guys also down there from Brighton. They became pals and spent time enjoying the various activities, such as football and water skiing and copious amounts of drinking at the various onsite pubs. They made friends with some of the Red Coats and Tigger took a shine to one particularly glamorous blonde, about six years older than him. He felt chuffed at the thought of an older woman getting romantic with him and at long last he was to lose his virginity! The one week stay ended up being two as he was having such a good time. The other two lads and Tigger used to take trips out of the Camp to visit areas around Minehead. The two weeks were over and Tigger offered to give the other two lads a lift back to Brighton. They all went to a party that evening and Tigger returned home the next day. He never saw the lads again.

Tigger's father was still feeling sorry about what happened to Tigger and Susan and sat him down one evening for a chat.

"I have been thinking about what happened between you and Susan. It is very unfortunate and sad what has happened but life goes on. You have been having one or two problems with your Ford and I have been thinking that maybe another car would be nice. A more up to date car? What do you think?"

"Well that sounds good but I cannot afford another car from my salary."

"Well, I know that so I am willing to lend you the money to buy another car and you can pay me back when you can. Maybe a little at a time – what do you think?"

"Gosh, Dad, that's very generous, have you seen anything that maybe good?"

"Well I have been to a garage in Worthing and they have a very nice ex-demonstration Mini – its blue with a white top."

They went over that weekend and had a test drive. The car was as new. Needless to say the car was bought and no sooner said than done, the new car was sitting on the driveway, Tigger could not wait to show his friends and have drives around the area, gleaming blue and white. It was the first time Tigger's father had done anything like this for him and he was very grateful. And Tigger's mother?

"Well I would not have done that if it had been left to me. Your dad has been too generous. You had better start paying back the money as soon as you can."

Chapter 21
A New Romance

One evening a number of months after his break up with Susan, a new girl appeared at Young Conservatives. An attractive blonde young lady whose parents had just moved down from the Birmingham area after her father's retirement from the Ministry of Transport Tigger and her started dating. She also worked in banking but at Lloyds Registrars Offices in Worthing. She also had a pony which she kept in a field at the local private girls school, West Preston Manor. Tigger knew nothing about horses at all but began to meet Mary at the school to help her, or at least be with her, when she groomed the pony.

After a while Tigger and Mary felt quite an attraction between them and they started dating more seriously. She let him ride her pony on odd occasions on the beach until one day the pony carted Tigger off along the beach. Luckily he did not come off!

After a number of months dating and the relationship becoming much more serious, Mr Grellier his manager summoned him into the office.

"Close the door, Warrington – I have some news for you which I hope you are going to like.

"I have a letter from head office. It is your first transfer. You have done well here but it is time for you to move on and advance your career. You may be surprised to hear they have given you a posting in Jersey in the Channel Isles. What do you think of that?"

"Well, I was expecting a move but not as far away as that."

"It would be a good move for you, get you away from home life and get you to stand on your own two feet, without your parents around you, be a feather in your cap. Now because it is such a move head office said they will give you a few days to think about it."

Part of him was feeling quite excited – Channel Isles, eh! But another part of him was thinking he would be away from months at a time from Mary and he was feeling quite an attraction to her.

That evening he met up with Mary and when Tigger told him his news she fell into floods of tears. Her father felt it would be a good career move for Tigger and anyway it would be a test for their relationship. Neither of her parents really wanted Mary to have a serious relationship and felt this move would, maybe, end it.

Tigger's parents opinions were mixed. His father thought it would be a good career move, whilst his mother felt he would not cope on his own, that he would go off the rails, just like his REAL mother. It would be the end of his affair with Mary.

Having mulled it over and talked for hours with Mary, Tigger made his decision. Monday morning and into Mr Grellier's office to tell him he would be turning down this lucrative move and he would be staying on the mainland.

"Pity, lad, it would have been the making of you – but it is your decision but expect another offer of a move very soon."

The rest of his colleagues in the office told him he was mad to turn down such a good offer. That he would have had the time of his life in Jersey.

Tigger himself was half regretting it and at times afterwards kicked himself for turning Jersey down. In his heart he really wanted to go. Life is a road we travel along and at times we get to a crossroads and wonder what direction to go. Left, right or straight on – this was one of those times and in hindsight Tigger took the wrong turning!

Before too long Mr Grelier was calling Tigger into his office again.

"Warrington – I told you another move offer would come soon. You are off to Goring Road Worthing as a cashier. Good luck, lad, and I hope you continue to do well."

He knew some of the staff at his new branch, in fact one of the girls was the sister of an old friend of Tigger at school. The manager was a decent enough chap but a bit of a snob, so not as good as Grellier. The chief clerk, Mr Brown, was an up and down sort of bloke who, at times, one did not know how to take on a daily basis. The rest were OK but there was not the atmosphere – was not a patch on Rustington. He continued with his evening classes and still found accounts THE most difficult subject to master. Law he liked the best. He found it to be quite stimulating. Exams were taken and he passed three at his first sitting. All five had to be passed in order to get a diploma.

As the months went by, work was OK and his relationship with Mary became more serious, until after much discussion they decided to get engaged, but first Tigger had to ask Mary's father for his daughters hand in marriage. Now he had a really good relationship with Susan's parents and found it easy when he asked for HIS permission to marry Susan. It was a different situation with Mary's father. They both knew that Mary's parents were not in favour of their serious relationship, so it was with some trepidation that Tigger met with her father to ask the question. He was very serious and pointed out that he and Mary's mother would feel happier if they gave it more time, they were not happy Tigger had turned down the Jersey move. He asked Tigger to speak to Mary with a view to thinking about marriage a little more before rushing into anything. Apparently the family had a long history of divorces and he did not want his daughter to go down that route! Mary's father even wrote a letter to Tigger's parents trying to persuade them to have a word with Tigger. None of these actions worked and Tigger and Mary, being both over 21 could get married without parents' permission.

Eventually wedding plans were made. Tigger's parents approached Mary's parents to help out both financially and arranging the wedding/reception. Their offer was promptly declined. There continued a rather uneasy atmosphere between Tigger and Mary's parents.

Chapter 22
The Wedding

The Atkinsons were quite a well off couple so they were going to see that their only daughter was to have a lavish, top hat and tails wedding and that no one else would be involved in the organisation.

Tigger's parents had again offered to help with the organisation but were politely and firmly told that their help would not be required. The only way that Tigger or his parents were to know what the arrangements were was through Mary. The marriage would take place in the local church. St Marys at East Preston, where Tigger had for so many years attended as an altar boy. The reception was at the largest hotel in Littlehampton, The Beach.

The principal guests were from the young Conservatives. Both Tigger and Mary had built up a good circle of friends from the Club. Best man Richard and bridesmaids, Mary Frampton and Anna Derrington Turner were in attendance. The honeymoon night was to be spent at a posh hotel in the New Forest followed by a week in the west country.

Before the wedding, Mary and Tigger had to find a place to live. Mary wanted to live in an old character house, but as these types of houses were completely out of their price range, a compromise had to be made and they plumped for a new house off north lane in Rustington – a three bedroomed mid terraced house with central heating. The bank gave them a loan at staff rates at interest only repayments. Having bought the house sometime before the wedding they both spent time painting and relaxing, they both wanted time alone away from parent domination!

By this time Mary's pony had given birth to a foal, it was a mystery how she became pregnant as there were few other horses or ponies around! Both her pony, Lassie and her foal were to attend the wedding and present Mary with a lucky horseshoe!

Come the day of the wedding, it turned out to be a lovely occasion and everything went smoothly. The weather was good, no one fluffed their lines and Tigger's mother did not make an embarrassment of herself. Tigger was pleased that his uncle Mike was able to come down from London where he now lived. It was a top hat and tails do and everyone looked good in their refinery – a bit too lavish for Tigger's liking! Speeches done and dusted, cake cut and upstairs to change ready for the off on honeymoon. No one knew where Mary's car was parked so no tin cans tied to the bumper or messages plastered to the back. So off they went and they were free at last to make their journey to the New Forest and then on to the west country.

It was very strange driving back knowing they were not going 'home' but to THEIR own home, a new house of their OWN. Having settled into their new home, with a mixture of new and second hand furniture, life settled down and both off to their respective jobs each day. As they both worked in Worthing they often shared transport. Although Mary had a good job at Lloyds Registrars her ultimate ambition was to have her own horse stables. Her own business. This ruffled a few 'feathers' with both parents, particularly Tigger's.

"What does she think she is doing wanting to give up a good well paid job to work with horses?" was Tigger's mother's comment.

Mary's father was more supportive and encouraged her to think long and hard about it before embarking upon such a change. Tigger had absolutely no experience of managing horses so would be of little or no help. Tigger remembers Mary's father telling her,

"I hope you make a real success of this new venture in your life and that you end up paying a lot of tax."

Strange, she thought, but then realised that what he meant was that the more tax she paid the more successful her business would be, little did she appreciate at the time that this would be her eventual downfall!

Soon weekends would be spent trawling around the countryside looking at prospective premises where she may be able to set up her business. Before too long she had heard about a local estate called Castle Goring. They went up there one weekend and found the place had some stables with a couple of horses already there. This was the beginning of a big life changing era in both Mary and Tigger's life.

Chapter 23
From Banking to Mucking Out

If Tigger was going to make a serious contribution to Mary's new venture he was going to have to learn how to ride. It was not good enough just to have a potter around on Mary's 12.2 hand pony. They knew one or two stables in the area, one of which was Joe Gilberts stables – The Pound in Angmering. She always had a horse or two for sale. Tigger took a shine to a young horse Joe had for sale, which she said was an ideal horse to learn to ride on. By this time Tigger and Mary had acquired the grazing rights on a field immediately opposite Tigger's parents' home, so the new horse and Lassie were kept there. The field was an ideal place for Mary to give Tigger some riding lessons.

It was a late afternoon in November when both of them were able to get away from work early and they decided to have a quick ride on the beach as the tide was out and before it got dark. They were both having a good canter along the sand. It was quite breezy, when suddenly Tigger's horse shied violently to one side from a piece of seaweed flapping in the wind. Bang. Tigger was off in an instant landing with a thud flat on the hard sand. The horse bolted off along the sand and up the beach along the road and over front gardens!

Meanwhile Tigger was staggering to his feet feeling very dazed, Mary having gone off to find his horse! He had hit the deck with such force that his jacket was split from the base to the collar and his riding hat was cracked to the crown. The horse had been caught. Tigger managed to climb back in the saddle and they ambled back to the field.

By the time they reached home all Tigger wanted to do was get to bed and go to sleep but he was speaking to Mary in a peculiar way and talking a load of rubbish she could not understand, walking around the bedroom bumping into the furniture. This worried Mary and she called the doctor. He was not long in arriving and immediately assessed Tigger, furious that Mary had not called an ambulance. Tigger had a delayed concussion! An ambulance was called and Tigger was taken to Worthing hospital where he was constantly asked questions, such as, his name, what day was it, his date of birth etc. All he wanted was to go to sleep but he was woken every half hour to be asked the same questions. The next day he was X-rayed and kept under observation. His mother and father came to visit and immediately his mother ranted about how he should not have been riding, he could not ride, she had had a premonition that he would fall off a horse and have a fatal head injury, all a ruse to get him to give up riding! They were to get rid of the horse. Tigger's father had to restrain his mother.

"He is not well, he is in hospital with a head injury and you should not be worrying him like this."

On the third day Tigger was discharged and he and Mary returned home. After a couple of further days off work he went to his doctor to get signed off so he could return to the bank.

"How you feeling? And how is your hip?"

"I am OK, why are you asking me about my hip?"

"Oh, did the hospital not tell you, apart from the concussion you have a cracked pelvis!"

"No I did not know that! What do I have to do?"

"Nothing much, just take it easy and lay off riding for a month or so."

Apart from being a little stiff for a while Tigger was back to normal in next to no time.

He and Mary spent weekends riding and being with their horses much to the dismay of Tigger's mother. She even tried to put Tigger off riding by telling him again she had a premonition that he would fall off a horse and have a fatal head injury. His father did not seem to be too worried about their new found interest and was quite laid back about it.

Mary and Tigger discussed a lot about the possibility of Mary leaving her job and Lloyds if she was able to get some stables at Castle Goring, it was a lifelong ambition to have her own stables and nothing was going to stop her.

They arranged to have a meeting with the landlord of Castle Goring, Fitzroy Somerset one Saturday. A tall man with a hair lip and well spoken. He and his family lived in an old Victorian house up a long drive off the A27. They made Mary and Tigger most welcome and after pleasantries they followed Mr Somerset upstairs to his office.

Mary explained that she and Tigger both currently worked in banks but that she had a lifelong ambition to have her own stables, that she had seen the group of building and stables on the south side of the estate and was there any possibility of her renting the stables and the grazing in the fields behind. Mr Somerset explained that he would consider the idea, but if he agreed he would wish Mary to have a successful business as that would reflect positively on his estate! He then suggested they all went over to see exactly what he could offer Mary and certain conditions he would require her to maintain.

There were four main stables, in good condition with solid Stafford stone floors and drainage. There were an assortment of other buildings in various states of repair. Behind were three or four paddocks. There was also an old cottage adjacent to the stables, which, at the time was not in the equation for rent.

Having spent quite some time looking over the place they said goodbye and Mr Somerset told them he would put something in writing about rent and tenure.

So it was the beginning of a change of life for them both, they hoped.

Tigger had, so far, in his life had a rather turbulent time and although married he did not feel at peace with his life. He was still sad that he had not had a family life that he would have wished for. He was never at ease with his mother, and there was very little, if any, love in the relationship. He had a better relationship with his father. He also missed Auntie Peta and often thought about his real parents.

But he regretted times when he felt his father should have backed him up or supported him when his mother was being so horrible to him. But what had gone was in the past. Tigger, granted, had learned good manners, respect and the value of money but what was sadly missing was the love that he had craved for with parents. Something that Auntie Peta had given him in the time he was at Horseshoe Lodge. Life is a journey along a road sometimes fraught with problems. Sometimes a crossroad is reached and a decision has to be made as to which direction you choose and Tigger was fast approaching that crossroad.

A few days after the visit to Castle Goring and the meeting with Fitzroy Somerset a letter dropped through the letter box for Mary. The letter outlined the terms and conditions of renting stables at Castle Goring. There would also be an opportunity to rent further buildings for conversion to stables subject to a satisfactory probation period during which Mary would have to prove to Mr Somerset that she was running a satisfactory business. Mary was delighted and she and Tigger then had the task of telling both sets of parents what they had decided to do. Her parents were full of support, her father telling her that he hoped that her business would be so successful she would have to pay a lot of tax! The more successful, the more tax would have to be paid. Little did he know how Mary would run her business!

As expected Tigger's parents were not so supportive, his mother even bluntly declaring that they were completely mad. Why was Mary giving up a perfectly good job to work with horses, and what did she know about horses anyway? Thanks for those few kind words!

Chapter 24
A Complete Life Change

Mary gave her notice to Lloyds Bank and set about planning her new life. Time at weekends was spent cleaning and painting up at the stables. Advertising in the West Sussex Gazette that a new livery stables was opening at Castle Goring which yielded some replies. The first girl to appear at the stables was Jessica Perkins, a schoolgirl who had a pony called Sugar. She decided to move her pony from where it was currently stabled and move to Castle Goring. Mary had her first livery. Jessica went to a local school in Worthing and had quite a few friends interested in horses, so they followed her to the stables, several volunteering to do work around the yard. In next to no time Mary had quite a number of liveries and it was apparent that she was fast running out of stables to house the new liveries. Tigger decided to have another meeting with Mr Somerset in which he put forward a suggestion that the various buildings around the stable that needed repairing to bring into use, that if Tigger were to do the necessary repairs that they could come to some agreement on a reduced rent. Somerset agreed to this and Tigger set about bringing several buildings back into use. There was The Old Coach House Flat with three stables on the ground floor that were of a good size and took little work to make them safe and comfortable for horses. He had no experience at all in this type of work but slowly and methodically he got the job done. This all had to be done at weekends as he was still working. There was another large building that was used partly for rearing of the pheasant chicks in incubators and another half of the building that had been used for the estates horses in the old days, lovely partitioned stables with Staffordshire stone block flooring and good drainage. The stables were open fronted as the horses were tethered at night, so these had to be modified to include adequate doors to keep the horses Mary had securely stabled.

Tigger was not as happy at the bank at Goring Road as he was at Rustington and after a year or so he had his next move to Pulborough, a country village by the River Arun. They were quite a nice bunch of people and he particularly liked the manager. The customers were predominantly wealthy, being located on the edge of mid Sussex. Big houses and racing stables, which meant big accounts and quite a busy branch. Tigger was now 2nd cashier/securities clerk. In those days banking was moving on apace and soon computers were being installed which was quite an interesting phase in Tigger's career. It also meant longer hours as much work was being done in preparation to the changeover to being completely computerised. All customers' details had to be logged on to the computer and they no longer were recognised by their names but by a NUMBER! Whilst this was progress and there was no stopping that, Tigger felt rather sorry for customers when he told them he no longer wanted their name to look up details of their account but a NUMBER! The hours got longer and at times Tigger was worried he might miss the last train home! The atmosphere in the branch became very strained at times with the enormous workload that they were all under and Tigger was enjoying his work less and less. The manager told him to bear with it as Tigger was destined for great things at the bank!

The stables was proving to be a success in quite a short time and Tigger and Mary had long discussions as to whether they could afford for Tigger to give up his career in banking and join Mary at the stables. He even had meetings with Mr Somerset to see what the possibilities were of him working on the Castle Goring Estate, maybe on a part time basis. Tigger and Mary also had to consider the mortgage on their house as, whilst working at the bank, they had preferential repayment rates. Taking everything into consideration they took an enormous gamble and decided to make the big move away from banking.

From that moment on their lives were to change forever.

Tigger's manager was extremely surprised by his decision to leave the bank and one he felt very ill advised. Tigger had a good career path mapped out and the bank had him marked as a high achiever and he would have gone on to high office. But his decision was made and his days in banking were over. The next big hurdle was telling both sets of parents, Tigger knew what the reaction would be from HIS parents and maybe Mary's parents would not be too happy either. Tigger never had a good relationship with his mother and his father had become rather 'distant' with him as well, so it was no surprise at the turbulent reaction he received when at last he told them he had already left the bank.

"Have you taken leave of your senses? We want nothing more to do with you, all that money we spent on your private education, always said it was the wrong decision to marry Mary, how are you going to make ends meet? Don't come to us when it all goes pear shaped and you run out of money etc etc."

It was indeed not only an exciting time but also very traumatic. He really did not want to fall out with his parents but he and Mary were determined to make a success of this new venture, you only live once so why not grasp the opportunity?

Tigger told them he did not want an argument, if it went wrong he could always re-apply to go back into banking but it was something he wanted to do – he loved the countryside and would do everything he could to make a success of his new life. After several further visits to his parents trying to convince them this is what he wanted he decided that if his visits to them were going to be so unpleasant and traumatic that there was no point in having any further contact with them until they were more pleasant to him. He was never to see his father again and his mother for several years. It seemed an awful thing to do but a parent/child relationship should be loving and joyful and if it were to be the complete opposite, what was the point of any relationship at all? Tigger was upset but had felt an enormous burden had been taken away from him. He had not seen Auntie Peta for some time but he wrote to her to tell her what he had done and he received a lovely letter in return supporting him in whatever he chose to do – a pity he had left the bank but it was his life to choose what he wanted to do.

Mary's parents were not so vocal in their disapproval of Tigger's decision to leave the bank but they did feel it was a bad decision. It was Mary's stables and Tigger should leave her to run her own business, however if that is the decision they had made jointly, they had to live with that. There would be an enormous amount of manual work to do around the stables which Mary would find difficult to do anyway and Tigger could not do it on a part time basis.

It was strange not getting ready for work in a suit, but instead in jeans and old work clothes. Tigger helped Mary around the stables, getting to know all the livery people, the horses and a new way of life. It soon became apparent, though, that travelling to and from their house in Rustington to Castle Goring every day was not ideal, leaving horses without anyone close by in case of a problem. There was also the problem of keeping up repayments on their house. The bank would not continue indefinitely with staff rates now Tigger had left. As previously mentioned, there was a cottage where the stable was situated which was now empty.

One evening some months later the phone rang and it was Aunt Evelyn from Leicester. By the tone of her voice something was wrong. Tigger knew that she did not approve of the new venture that he and Mary were about to embark on but it was not that.

"Michael, your father is gravely ill in hospital, it would be good if you could go and see him, remember he thinks a lot of you and I would not like to think anything happens and you did not see him for one last time."

It was a shock for Tigger and quite unexpected. He had often wanted to meet up with his father and try and smooth things over but never plucked up the courage to do so.

He would see his father at the weekend and try and make peace with him but two days later before he had a chance to go to the hospital Aunt Evelyn rang again to break the news that his father had died. Tigger would forever regret that he never said goodbye to his father.

With a very heavy heart Tigger made the short journey to see his mother. The meeting was not as traumatic as he had anticipated but it was not long before his mother was taunting him and blaming him for his father's illness. Tigger had to take it. It was a very sad time and not the occasion to start rowing.

His father had had a heart attack and various other health issues and he had rapidly gone downhill. Tigger had not expected this otherwise he would have immediately gone to visit him in hospital and not wait for the weekend!

The funeral was arranged and relatives from Leicester came down. Uncle Arnold was Tigger's father's brother, a really nice man who was a sympathetic ear for Tigger. Father's side of the family had experienced his mother's sharp tongue on many an occasion so knew exactly what Tigger had been going through. They knew why he had run away from home when he was at school. Uncle Arnold thought it odd Tigger and Mary had given up good jobs, but wished them well and hoped they made a success of the business.

Tigger continued to see his mother for some time after his father's death but eventually visiting her became unbearable with constant rows and horrible accusations, so once again Tigger ceased to have any contact. It was his life and if his mother could not accept that then there was no point in having any contact. Life is too short for the continual hassle and unpleasantness, he felt he had to stand up for himself and not be influenced by his mother any more. She had ruled his life, he had been treading on eggshells for too many years, it was time to break free!

A further meeting with Mr Somerset proved very fruitful and resolved many of their potential problems. Mr Somerset purchased their Rustington house, leaving them with a few thousand pounds profit in the bank. They both then moved into the old stable cottage dating from the 1700s – No. 13! Mr Somerset provided them with a new kitchen and a few new windows. They were now living on the premises which was a great relief to them both.

The cottage was quite roomy with four bedrooms, a lounge, dining room and another room, which they called 'Out the Back'. It was by the back door and where they were able to keep much of their own personal horse saddlery and of course there was a kitchen and bathroom, NO central heating, only a back boiler heated from the open fire and quite a large garden, where they would grow vegetables and have chickens.

Chapter 25
The Business Grows

Tigger never heard from his mother except for the odd Christmas card on which she could not even put 'love, from Mother', but put 'From C Warrington'! And he had to live with that. He had been fed up with a lifetime of arguments, snide remarks and a seemingly total lack of affection. He felt a coldness towards her now. He also had a letter from his aunt in Leicester telling them what a bad decision he had made and it was about time he made it up with his mother but it takes two to tango! If his life was to be bearable and was to be a success in the new stables venture then Tigger needed a complete break from his mother which was the only way forward and he felt a sense of relief and release. He missed his father and always regretted not seeing him before he died – but if Tigger was to make a change it had to be complete. The shackles were off and he had freedom to do what he liked without having to be accountable to his mother.

The two of them soon settled into their new lifestyle. A hard life seven days a week but never a dull moment. Tigger was learning to ride to a good standard, having professional lessons from good horse people and he in turn was able to give lessons to pupils at the stables. Money was tight and Tigger was not convinced that Mary was running the money side of the stables in a very efficient way, but when he queried this with Mary, he was told not to worry she was sorting things out. He never saw any correspondence from HMRC or National Insurance which concerned Tigger.

Eventually Tigger got a full time job on the estate. Mr Somerset was re-evaluating the farming side of the estate and appointed an estate manager – Ron Lampshire plus one or two others including Tigger. Being a complete novice to a farming way of life and farm machinery, Tigger knew he had an enormous amount to learn and quickly in order to establish himself as a useful member of the farm team. He took to it like a duck to water and was soon able to be trusted to drive large tractors, operate ploughs, baling machines and all the other pieces of land equipment. Tigger quickly got to know every inch of the estate, both fields and woodland and he soon became very good at his job. He loved it and felt very much at ease and at home. Life was becoming very good. Evenings were spent at the local pub, The Coach and Horses with other men who worked on the estate playing darts, general chat and banter, the pub was within walking distance of the cottage. There were a mixed bunch of people living on the estate and some interesting characters. There was Mick, known by some as the Abo, as he had the features of an Australian Aboriginal! Nigel and Bert, all three were good mates who often went fishing for cod and supplied local hotels and restaurants. Mike, a lad who lived away from the estate, Dave Chalk (Chalky) who drove the bulldozer on the estate tip, a student and Tigger. There were two separate farms on the estate, Holt Farm where Mr Somerset lived and Northdown Farm where the milking herd was located and the cowman lived in a cottage on the farm – there were also two other tenant farms. It was not a huge estate but enough to keep everyone busy, with a mixture of the milking herd, beef stock with wheat and barley as the arable side.

Close by the stable a single girl lived in a mobile home, Lyn, known as Dim Lyn, a lovely girl and not really dim but the name stuck for some reason. She worked at a local Bookies so not at all dim, however she did come out with some classic tales or one liners at times. She struck up a good friendship with Tigger and Mary and was always popping down the stables for a chat and a cuppa. On one such occasion she was chatting about an old boyfriend, Tony remarking that he had been married but got a 'quick' divorce as the married had never been constipated!!! And on another occasion Tigger could help to put together an advert for a pony she had, for the West Sussex Gazette,

"You are better at these things than me as I am a bit illegitimate!!!"

Ron Lampshire was a tough guy who did not suffer fools gladly but he was generally a fair man and trusted Tigger to do a variety of jobs around the estate, including the use of a chain saw. He occasionally let off steam if he felt the workers were not pulling their weight and Tigger often fired back if he felt Ron was being unfair. Ron seemed to respect this and at times even received an apology! Tigger soon learned that at times country folk fired off, as it were, but generally all was soon forgotten and life carried on. It was a hard and at times, a tough life, but most of the time everyone got on well with one another in and out of work and they could all rely on one another for favours if needed. Evenings were often spent at the local pub, The Coach and Horses where a lot of tales were told and pub games.

One of the perks of working on an estate is that those who lived there were entitled to wood for their fires in the home and when winter was approaching they all took it in turns at weekends to cut down trees or where there were fallen trees and branches, load up a trailer and drop it off at their houses, ready for chopping into logs, providing enough to carry them over the winter. Tigger was good with a chainsaw and very safety conscious. There had been a violent storm in recent days and Tigger and another worker, Dave, were on one of their wood cutting forays in an area called The Chestnuts. There were large fallen branches all over the place, some stuck in the forks of other branches. Dave was cutting off one such branch and with each cut the branch fell nearer to the ground, when suddenly, high up in the main tree, a large branch broke off, tumbling towards the ground it struck Tigger fair and square across his head. Luckily he fell to the side of his chainsaw with blood pouring from a large head wound. It took a minute or two for Dave to realise what had happened as he had his back to Tigger. Tigger was in and out of consciousness but with the help of Dave, managed to stagger to the nearby gate on the main road, where luckily another one of the estate workers was driving by. He stopped and rushed Tigger to hospital to be treated and have fourteen stitches inserted! Apart from being a bit sore Tigger was none the worse for wear, the real thing that made him 'sore' was the phone call he received that evening from another stable owner nearby asking him if he could ride one of his clients horses at The Horse of the Year Show the following day. What an opportunity which he had to turn down because of his head injury. It proved how far Tigger had come when he was getting such good offers and it showed the respect he was getting from fellow horse riders.

Mary's own pony was now living up at Castle Goring and was getting on in years. It was a purebred Exmoor Pony, which in those days had to be branded on the shoulders and the rump to prove they were purebred. Mary had managed to buy two more Exmoors and the loan of a stallion, Luckwell and before long a beautiful colt was born, the first at the stables. They named him Acorn. The other two purebred mares were good ponies and they were soon entered into local and county shows. Of course there were other horses and ponies to be looked after at the stables. Early morning mucking out and feeding. All the usual stable duties. By this time there were quite a few regular girls at the stables at weekends and at school holiday time. They all got on well together, became interested in the shows and how the ponies performed. A deal was struck that if the girls managed to get up to the stables in the early morning, muck out two or three stables each then they could go to the shows with Tigger and Mary. When they returned from the shows they had to help bed the horses down for the night. By now Mary and Tigger had an old Mark 1 Land Rover and a horse trailer. When entering a show one had an exhibitors badge and one grooms badge, so when there were three or four of the girls going to the shows, as they neared the showground they had to travel in the trailer with the ponies so they were unseen at the showground entrance! Many times Jessica was one of the 'chosen' girls!

They generally did well at all the shows they went to and soon Tigger and Mary had quite a collection of rosettes and were getting a good name for themselves. With this growing success in mind Mary decided it was time to try entering the bigger shows. As Acorn was growing into a fine young colt and Lucky, his father, not having been shown for some years. An ideal show to enter was The Ascot Stallion Show at Ascot Racecourse. Both animals were well prepared for the show and looking good with excellent coats. They had new show bridles with brass buckles. Tigger was charged with showing Acorn as he was a lively character. His class was first and he showed himself off perfectly. He was pulled out first with the judge praising his condition and behaviour. Lucky (Luckwell) was up next and he won his class! Unbelievable, how pleased was Tigger and Mary? Having won both their classes, this qualified them for the championship and they BOTH won their respective championships. As an added bonus, the whole episode was being filmed for a TV programme! Unfortunately they never did see this programme as it was being televised whilst they were out working in the stables! There were plenty of photographers around from all the horsey magazines, the most notable of which was The Horse and Hound.

One can only imagine the reception they received on their return to the stables. Local stables in the area had been somewhat suspicious of these two new people who had opened up stables at Castle Goring but now there was a good acceptance that THEY HAD ARRIVED!

So much so that one morning a large envelope arrived in the post inviting them both to the Horse of the Year Show Ball at The London Hilton! They booked into a hotel near The Hilton, having driven up to the city in their Mark 1, rather decrepit Land Rover, to be hidden in the hotel underground car park. The Ball went on all night finishing with a lavish morning breakfast.

Returning to Castle Goring it was back down to earth, but they felt proud to have been invited to such a prestigious event and rubbing shoulders with the top British and overseas horse folk.

By now both Mary and Tigger were gaining a lot of respect from all the local stables in the area and were often invited to the weekend parties. They all worked hard and also played very hard, sometimes hardly remembering how they got home at night! Mary and Tigger were known locally as Tom and Jerry, which from then on was what everyone called them!

More shows were to be attended with continued successes, at Guildford Town Show, Surrey County, The Three Counties Show, Southern Counties Show at Ardingley and The Royal Windsor. In between Tigger had to work on the farm!

Life seemed to be going at ninety miles an hour. Winters were often hard and water pipes froze even in the house. Life was tough but they were young and took all things in their stride. During the winter months with few shows to go to, Tigger arranged different winter activities on horseback that not only the clients at the stables could join in but local riders from the other stables. He arranged events such as treasure hunts, timed rides and mock hunts – all very enjoyable and it kept a good continuity going amongst the local riding community.

Summer though was the time when life was really at its best, with a mixture of hard work and play.

Tigger was working hard on the farm and enjoying himself. Getting up at 4 a.m. to mow fields of grass ready for harvesting in the afternoon. At harvest time baling all the straw and then ploughing ready for next year's crop. Back at the stables after a day's work on the estate there was more work to be done at the stables, either riding out or stable or field maintenance. On long hot summer evenings when everyone had finished their work and the horses were all bedded down for the night, quite often a spontaneous water fight happened! Buckets of water over everyone, letting off steam and all their dogs joined in!

During the autumn/winter months Tigger went on the Saturday Estate Pheasant Shoots, with the team of beaters, often taking his beloved dog Heidi with him. Very tiring but so enjoyable. At times Tigger was the picker up, collecting all the shot pheasants and hanging them on the gun cart. He met all the guns, who were all very wealthy men with varying professions, from vets, solicitors to magistrates and owners of large land estate companies. One of the guns was also a keen amateur photographer and often gave Tigger excellent photos of the days shoot.

Tigger's life was a very fast learning curve. He was getting fit, learning about country life and people from all walks of life in the horse world. He was also learning about being competitive, riding horses to quite a high standard. He was very interested in show jumping and cross country riding. Mary was more cautious and had a leaning towards dressage, which Tigger had little interest in or the patience! Their relationship with Mr Somerset continued to be good and Tigger became responsible for all the stables, which included field and fence maintenance. He was always doing something after finishing work on the farm, rolling, harrowing or fertilising the twenty acres of fields. They had two main fields, a small paddock for older horses and the bottom field for schooling and show jumping. Tigger, though, wanted to expand the business even further. More stables were needed, which was Marys part of the business, but Tigger wanted to have an annual show in one of the fields and also to construct a good cross country course. Each year Tigger and Mary went to the Badminton Horse Trials and he always took a sketchbook to take down ideas for fences that he could reconstruct on a smaller scale back home. Armed with all his ideas he presented them to Mr Somerset, who, with a little persuasion, went along with the ideas. He always wanted something like this on the estate and as long as the organisation was good and it put the Castle Goring Estate on the map and in a good light, he supported what Tigger had in mind. In return Tigger would have use of a tractor, trailer, timber from the woods for the fences and the farm JCB Digger to dig holes to make the fences solid and to move soil and equipment; and a chainsaw, all this at weekends or evenings when not needed by the farm. Mr Somerset would present all the trophies and rosettes, plus he would donate a cup, The Fitzroy Somerset Cup for the Open Cross Country Class.

The first summer show was a huge success and competitors came from near and far. A good time was had by all.

Over the months a good solid cross country course was designed, constructed and Mr Somerset even allowed part of the course to go through the woods. He invited Mr Somerset to walk the course with Tigger to make sure everything met with his approval, congratulations were in order! Many of the fences could be seen from the start/finish line which made it a good spectator event. The event was always held in September, a month when the weather was most reliable and the harvest completed and so it was to prove that way. Again this event was very well supported with up to 100 competitors taking part, everyone having a marvellous time. Hard, hard work but well rewarded. *Next year would be even better*, Tigger thought.

The summer of 1976 was to be one of the driest on record. There had been no rain for months and the heat was so intense that the horses had to be brought in to the stables during the day to avoid the sun. Some horses do get sun stroke and so creams had to be administered. A wary eye also had to be kept on the fields in case of fire, the ground was so dry. Enormous cracks appeared and the animals had to be given hay as the grass was in such short supply. On the farm it was impossible to do any ploughing or sowing of crops so Mr Somerset decided to have all his workers resurrect an old lake on the estate. It was overgrown with reeds, shrubs and willow. A large digger and four dumper trucks were hired and from dawn to dusk they worked on clearing out the old lake. By September the job was complete and the day they finished the rains returned and the lake was soon full of water and to be stocked with trout for a private trout fishing group for Mr Somerset's wealthy friends. A good job done and work soon returned to the farm.

The Cross Country Event that year went ahead as there had been enough rain to make the ground safe. Tigger had constructed new and more solid fences and the Open Course had around 25 fences. The event was indeed a bigger success, with high class competitors. The Open Event being won by

Josh Gifford's wife Althea Gifford, mother of the now Olympic Rider Tina Gifford. Tigger had managed to get the whole day sponsored by various local companies and by the more wealthy clients at the stables who had businesses.

Tigger and Mary were enjoying life but were they really enjoying each other's company? Mary was increasingly away from home taking part in dressage competition on her new horse and new expensive Stuben German dressage saddle which was making Tigger increasingly worried that Mary was spending above her means. The prize money at these events was not good and he still had the niggling feeling Mary was not keeping good books for the business. More stables were needed as more people wanted to keep their horses at Castle Going Stables, an ideal location for riding and with lovely grazing fields, good shows and of course The Cross Country Course! Another meeting with Fitzroy Somerset was needed to persuade him that a new stable block was needed. He was pleased at the way the stables were being run, events that were held were successful, so he was happy to sanction a new block of eleven stables. In order to keep costs down Mr Somerset agreed to let Tigger use the estate's bulldozer to level and prepare the ground where the new stables were to be situated. More staff were needed and so Tigger and Mary had two live in girls in addition to Jessica who had been with them from the start. The new stables arrived together with a team of men who were to erect them all in a day. The new block of stables looked smart and many of the girls wondered whether their horse would get a new home! With these new stables the whole business now had around 35 stables dotted around the place.

Tigger competing on Polo at a local horse trial

By this time, Tigger had a lifetime loan of an ex Grade B showjumper horse called Polo, a white grey, and Mary had another horse which it was her intention to bring up to a good dressage standard and also maybe to show as a show cob. There were also one or two other horses that were at livery at the stables, which were good at either show jumping or cross country.

and on another horse, Carwyn

Tigger was competing at evening indoor shows in the winter after he had finished work. A group from the stables would go to Frensham in Hampshire in a large horse box, where they could also have a meal whilst watching the jumping. Tigger usually did quite well riding either Polo or Carwyn.

Mary's new horse, a chestnut mare, was not that good at dressage so Tigger rode her in show cob classes at various shows including Hickstead, where many international horse shows are held. It was good to compete and see all the world's top show jumpers and show riders.

On one such visit to Hickstead, Tigger was standing next to Harvey Smith, the well-known and famous international show jumper, at the entrance to the main arena, Harvey was waiting to 'walk the course' – Tigger asked him how he thought he was going to get on today?

"Well, young man, put it this way, I do not go into competitions to come second!"

A typical comment from a Yorkshire farmer and one Tigger would never forget!

Tigger competed in the Main International Arena and although he never won he was usually in the top three. On one occasion whilst Mary was watching Tigger compete, she met up with Sue Bunn, the wife of the then owner of Hickstead, who had a horse for sale. Mary ended up buying the horse, Gold Erodian (Roddy for short) a part bred Arab. She was hoping it would make a good dressage horse. Now Tigger was not a fan of 'pretty' Arabs but this horse was a bit special and was an absolute joy to ride. After sometime training at home it was quite apparent that Roddy was not going to make the grade in dressage, so it was plan B showing. Tigger's standard of riding had improved so much that any horse in the stable that was of showing standard, Tigger was your man to take it to the shows to stand a good chance of coming away with a rosette!

Roddy was taken to quite a few shows and there were few that he did not come home the winner. One of the livery owners at the stables had expressed a keen interest in Roddy and had often watched Tigger schooling him in the field. His daughter had a pony at livery with Mary and he had wanted his own horse as his daughter's pony was a little small for him. A good deal was done and Roddy changed owners and Tommy Harrison had his horse. The conditions of sale were that, Roddy would remain at livery at Castle Goring and that if Tommy wanted him shown then Tigger would ride for him. Tommy certainly was not up to showing Roddy at Arenas such as Hickstead. Tommy was an ex jockey and had no finesse when it came to knowing how to show a horse off to its best ability.

Life continued at a great pace and Mary and Tigger seemed to have less and less quality time together. Mary fell asleep after the evening meal in front of the log fire whilst Tigger went to the pub.

Tigger's time seemed to be spent equally between working on the farm and work at the stables. He was in the prime of his life, fit as a fiddle and not an ounce of fat on him and loved spending time improving the stables, repairing and maintaining the fields, fencing and tending the fields. Some of the girls at the stables often helped him and he was flattered by their attention. I guess he was a successful rider in their eyes and liked to hang around with him. Competitions at weekends came and went until Tommy was approached about entering Roddy into an event at Hickstead – The Ridden Part Bred Arab Class. This was quite a prestigious event and Tigger wanted to be well prepared.

The day of the show arrived and Tigger chose four of the girls at the stable he thought would be the best to help him at the showground. They arrived in plenty of time only to find the judge had brought forward the event time as he wanted to get away to another appointment! The last thing Tigger wanted to do was rush his preparations, however the judge was prepared to wait for late arrivals. Tigger entered Ring Three, immaculately turned out. He did his walk, trot, canter, gallop and back to walk without a hitch. Roddy was very responsive to leg commands and was like riding a Rolls Royce with four legs! The judge had a young assistant who then rode Roddy so the judge could see how he performed for a stranger. Perfect! The saddle was then removed and Tigger had to run him up and down to see whether he trotted evenly. Perfect! Saddle back on and Tigger remounted whilst the judge contemplated his decision. He bought Roddy out first, much to the dismay of another lady competitor!

"I usually win," she told Tigger.

"I am sorry, but I cannot help it if the judge prefers my horse, maybe you should take it up with him?"

The first and second placed horses qualified for the championships in the international ring in front of the grandstands with thousands of spectators watching.

"What chance do I stand, as I came second? There is no point in going into the main ring," said the woman.

So Tigger and Roddy strode into the international arena along with Arabs and part bred Arabs from other classes. Tigger felt both nervous and proud. Roddy, as usual, performed without putting a foot wrong, Tigger even managed to get an extended trot all the way past the grandstand to much applause from the crowd. All the horses lined up in the centre of the ring, the judges taking their final look at the horses before making their decision and then Tigger saw the principle judge give him the nod. He had won, he had a championship at Hickstead in the international arena. He received several rosettes. The sponsorship, the winner and the championship, a wonderful long red white and blue rosette with a gold centre. He was off cantering around the arena, rosettes blowing in the wind, receiving loud applause. How good did that feel? When he got outside all the girls crowded round some in tears. There were photographers and even one or two youngsters wanting Tigger's autograph! Tommy Harrison could not attend so would be extremely pleased and surprised at such a great win when they returned home. He always took the rosettes and gave them to his daughter, so Tigger was determined not to show Tommy ALL the rosettes won, only a selected few and he certainly was not going to let his daughter have the Championship rosette, something he treasures even today. This was indeed the highlight of his career with horses. Once back at the stables everyone came out to greet their triumphant return. Tommy was elated and full of congratulations. His win was to open yet another door.

One day when Tommy was up at the stables he had just finished his ride on Roddy and told Tigger there was something he wanted to discuss with him. They wandered off down the fields in order to be away from eager ears. Tommy was impressed with the way Tigger rode Roddy and with his win at Hickstead was just the icing on the cake. He had been thinking about taking things a little further and put it to Tigger that he would like to have a show jumping horse and would like Tigger to ride for him. Tigger pointed out that whilst he was flattered and excited by the idea, Tommy thought through all the costs. Tigger would be happy to try and find a suitable horse and ride for him but was not prepared to stump up any of the running costs. Apart from the initial cost of the horse there was the livery costs, all the tack, vet and farrier bills plus costs of entering the various shows. Tommy was quite happy to go along with all the costs. The matter of money cleared up. Tigger had to have a budget for this new horse. Between 2000 and 3000 pounds. Tigger knew exactly the person who would be able to find him a suitable horse, Jabina Maslin with whom he had riding lessons. Jabina was on the fringes of the

England Show Jumping Team and was in an ideal position to put some feelers out to find a suitable young horse. So it was to be. A phone call from Jabina one day said she thought she had found the ideal horse. The current owner was taking the horse to a Sunday indoor show at Frensham Ponds, just inside the Hampshire border. So off he went to see whether this horse would be a suitable candidate! He met the owners and Jabina who were there to see how Tigger and the horse got on together.

Tigger rode the horse in the practice area, took him over a few fences and got on fine. Jabina felt there was a good partnership in the making. Tommy was there and he liked the look of the horse, a good solid 16.1hh. A deal was done and Tigger took Heron back to his new home at Castle Goring. He was a big strong horse, a four year old. Tommy was over the moon with his new horse and gave Tigger carte blanche to do what he liked with Heron.

He was registered with the British Show Jumping Association as The Coppersmith as a Grade C Showjumper.

A busy time ahead, with the usual 'getting to know you' period, schooling, getting familiar with all the other horses at the stable and then deciding which shows to enter Heron. It was winter time so plenty of time for preparation for the outside shows in the spring and summer time. Schooling went well and Tigger took Heron over a few of the cross country fences around the fields. He was certainly a strong horse, enjoyed his work and Tigger certainly had his work cut out controlling him and schooling him. All was going so well. Mary seemed pleased for Tigger but she had her own dressage competitions to concentrate on. Tigger often felt she was a little jealous of the attention Tigger was getting and the success he was making of his riding. Of course he still had a job on the farm which took up most of the day time hours as well as fitting in riding and weekend competitions with other horses of his own.

Tigger had growing concerns that Mary was not running the financial side of her business in a proper fashion, something that was increasingly worrying him. This increased one day when Tigger took a phone call from her horse feed supplier asking when she was going to pay a large outstanding bill. This caused a row between them but she told Tigger it was a mistake and she had matters in hand, it was nothing to do with him, anyway! Tigger did not believe her. She had this habit of rubbing her nose when she was lying!

Chapter 26
Heron Goes Show Jumping

Heron's time had come. Summer was fast approaching and Heron was jumping well and he was entered for his first registered class at a local show at Angmering. There were 48 entered and Tigger figured that Heron would have to do pretty well to get anywhere near a top place against some really stiff competition. The course was quite challenging but he performed well and only had one refusal which Tigger put down to himself not being forceful enough, he was however more than pleased with the round. It was quite extraordinary that there were only three clear rounds in the class so Heron ended up 4th which was quite amazing for such a novice horse to do so well.

Heron competing in his first show.

Further shows were to follow and although he never won he was always in the top four. Tommy was more than happy with how things were panning out. He never rode Heron out of the stables himself as he was a small man and Heron would have just run away with him.

Herons schooling continued, he joined in the rides out with other horses from the stable and always wanted to be the lead horse. He was a joy to ride and a lovely bond developed between him and Tigger.

Jumping at a show at Goodwood

Tigger was still riding Mary's Show Cob at shows – Cindy, short for Cincinnati and although she did quite well at the shows rarely did she excel and get a first. Mary, however, was convinced she would come good. Cindy was a chestnut mare and prone to bouts of bad temperament, not a good attribute for showing. She was entered for the Horse of the Year Show at Wembley. Tigger was not in favour of her being entered as the competition would not only be from UK based horses but also from abroad.

The day came and off to London they went. A lovely day and a long wait for the cob class. Cindy was in her stable with the sun blazing down and she was very relaxed, in fact TOO relaxed!!! The time came for them to go into the ring outside and it was obvious Cindy needed some waking up!

'Give her the stick' was the advice from some other competitors, but Tigger was not into any beatings, relying on his own ability and riding to get her going. After an age, as there were quite a number of competitors the judge lined up, those he wanted to go forward to the international arena inside Wembley, Cindy was not included. Tigger would have been surprised had she been called forward. You cannot win them all but it was slightly disappointing as Tigger would have loved to have gone into the Wembley Arena but it was not to be. So they packed up and went home.

Tigger was also enjoying his work on the farm and he was given many different responsibilities. Life continued to be good. So it came as a complete shock to him as well as the other farm workers when one morning Ron Lampshire, the farm manager had a meeting with them all to say that Fitzroy Somerset was going through a tough time and he was going to have to make some redundancies as the farm was losing money. There were to be three of them who would be losing their jobs. Tigger immediately had that gut feeling he was to be one of the three. And so it was to be. Fitzroy Somerset went round one evening to see Tigger at the cottage with a brown envelope which was the formal notice of redundancy. He was so sorry to lose Tigger being such a good worker but felt Tigger would be able to join forces with Mary in her business. Tigger was devastated, he had never experienced redundancy or being out of work. It was then that the true reality of how Mary's business was being run came home to roost. There was no way that Tigger and she could join forces in running the stables. Mary had not been paying bills. Money was owed not only to her food suppliers but to the farrier and to the vets. It was a terrible shock and one that was to have a devastating effect upon their relationship. There was, all of a sudden, a rather sad and subdued atmosphere around the stables, the girls and clients felt so sorry for Tigger and some of them were aware things were far from rosy between him and Mary.

One of the clients said to Tigger,

"Try to keep your chin up, one door closes and another will open."

How true it was to be but at the time Tigger could not see it that way.

So Tigger had to find another job. After the initial shock he decided he had to get on with it. Moping around would achieve nothing. He found work at the local racing stables in Findon with the famous race horse trainer, Capt Ryan Price. He had never ridden a race horse before, let alone riding so short in the stirrups. However they were very accommodating and after a slow start on a late developing horse he was soon riding good horses. It was hard work with early morning starts at around 5.30 and two or maybe three rides. The money was poor and soon Tigger was realising he could not survive on such low pay. The head lad, Con Horgan, wanted Tigger to stay on, manage the gallops and help some of the young lads with their riding but with little or no increase in pay. Tigger reluctantly could not commit to this.

After a few short but enjoyable months Tigger decided he had to find another job that paid a better wage. He had been out of the work place for jobs suitable for his qualifications for some years now and going back into banking or a professional job was not going to be easy. He applied for several jobs with farming connections such as pest control and a rep for a weed killer/fertiliser company without success. He ultimately took a job on a milk round in Littlehampton, which paid quite good money, if one worked at it as there were bonuses to be earned for promoting food products other than milk. It was an early start but an early finish for five days of the week. Friday and Saturday longer as money had to be collected!!! So Tigger was able to continue with his riding and his competitions.

Heron and Tigger built a good partnership, competing at many local shows both indoor and outdoor where Heron gained more and more experience. They competed once at a show at Ardingley, the south of England Showground, where he competed against Marion Mould, who rode for Great Britain, she also had a young horse. Tigger and Heron came 3rd beating Marion!!! Tigger continued with his training of Heron and one quiet evening he went down to the jumping paddock and eventually plucked up the courage to build a five feet parallel fence. At first Heron knocked it down, he did not refuse the fence rebuilt, he gathered his composure and Tigger faced Heron to the fence once more and what a sheer delight as Heron cleared it perfectly without even touching a pole. Tigger knew then Heron could really jump.

Tigger was also able to run the stables annual show and cross-country event, which he was able to again get sponsorship from local companies and some of the liveries owners who had their own businesses. These shows yielded quite a good amount of money which helped with outstanding bills.

Tigger was angry and worried about Mary's lack of business acumen and the fact that she was lying to Tigger about the finances of the business. He was pretty sure she was not paying any national insurance for the girls she employed or completing any tax returns and yet she was buying expensive German Stubben saddles and bridles for her dressage horse. She was not having much success with her competitions either. In truth she was not a very competent rider and lacked a degree of confidence. Things were to go from bad to worse.

Chapter 27
The Final Breakup

Whilst Tigger was working hard on his milk round he knew that things had to change. He could not continue a life working at such a job and things were only going one way with him and Mary. He continued to ride and compete in evening shows but his heart was not in it as it used to be. Having a job away from the stables, a relationship that was seriously on the rocks, he soon realised that something had to give. He was having a social life outside of his marriage, he was meeting some of his milk round ladies who were more interested in his horse life than Mary was. After a series of disagreements and rows things came to a final head. They argued over the way Mary was running the business with little or no accounts, paying no tax and national insurance, getting into debt with so many people, life was becoming extremely stressful and unbearable. They had drifted so far apart that they had only stayed together because of their lifestyle and had little time for one another for a long time. Things finally came to a head and Mary wanted Tigger out of the house and out of her life. This was sudden and Tigger knew that the inevitable was coming but did not contemplate such an abrupt end. What was he to do, where was he going to live? He had very little money, in fact he had less than 50 pounds to his name He was desperate. With a heavy heart and with much reluctance he wrote to his mother and told her the predicament he was in. They agreed to meet. Tigger knew he would have to face an enormous amount of nagging and rows with his mother but he had no alternative other than to be on the streets. Penniless and homeless!!! It could have happened so quickly.

How quickly things can change in life. Tigger was at rock bottom in his life. He was in a state of utter despair with no one he could out pour his feelings. He really should have had professional counselling but in those days it was not readily available. At the time he did not appreciate that this was to be a turning point in his life. The previous years since he had left his banking career had been hard but it certainly made him mature into a man. In later years he would appreciate, also, that this period in his life was a solid foundation building time for what the future held for him. Those years taught him about hard work, never giving up and about people from all walks of life. Now was the time he had to dig deep and get himself out of this dreadful situation.

His mother reluctantly agreed he could stay back at the bungalow in his old cramped room but that he would have to pay his way. She had little money and could not afford to subsidise his food and lodgings, so she said. She charged Tigger about 30 pounds a week, quite a lot in the late 70s/80s. He suffered an enormous amount of nagging but made sure he was either out every night at the Coach and Horses or went to bed. He was drinking too much at the pub but it was helping to drown out what was going on in his torrid life at the time. As time went on he met up with Mary to settle what was going to happen and who was going to instigate divorce proceedings. They ended up with Mary paying for the divorce which was completed very quickly. No children or property involved or finances to be settled. Just his lovely Labrador dog Heidi. It was decided she could stay at the stables where she would be happy but miss Tigger. He would go up and regularly take her for walks. Things seemed to settle down a little. That was until one day Tigger had a letter from the Inland Revenue to say HE owed quite a sum to the Revenue. Mary had not been paying any tax or national insurance as he had suspected all along. As he and Mary had been married she was his responsibility. He had no money to pay the bill or money to fight his case via a solicitor. He decided to grab the bull by the horns and book an appointment to see someone from the Revenue. As it happens a nice chap who, when Tigger explained the stables was not HIS business but Mary's, decided to be lenient towards Tigger and made the decision to write the debt off in Tigger's name and they would sort it out with Mary. One less thing to worry about. What an enormous relief.

Tigger decided he had to get on with life and decided on his limited resources and money to start to enjoy life. He had to first tell Tommy Harrison that he could no longer ride for him and he would have to make other arrangements. That was a tough thing for Tigger to have to do and he felt sorry for Tommy. But Tommy was very understanding and they parted company on the best of terms. Heron was eventually sold to a girl who could not ride one side of Heron and eventually and very sadly Heron's jumping days were over. Tigger felt very deflated that only a short while ago he was enjoying life to the full, successful in all he was doing and now he was at the bottom of the ladder trying to climb his way back up. How the mighty fall?

Tigger had a series of lady friends, some from his milk round connections and some from people at the Coach and Horses. At least life was now not as bad as it had been a short while ago. One evening at The Coach and Horses he was having a drink with Martin, The Castle Goring Keeper of the Shoot.

"So sorry to hear about Heidi, she was a lovely dog!"

"What are you on about, Martin?"

"Has Mary not told you? Heidi wandered on to the main road outside the stables, suspect she was looking for you when she got knocked over and killed. I am so sorry, no idea you did not know."

"God, no, I had no idea. No one has told me. The bitch, why would Mary have not told me?"

Tigger was really upset. As if things were not bad enough for him. Heidi was the most devoted and loyal dog he had ever had. He obviously gave Mary a piece of his mind!

He was making up for many lost years of good female company. But he could not continue doing his milk round job or flitting from one lady friend to another. He wanted to settle down again and have a truly loving and strong relationship.

He hated having to live with his mother and more especially as she now had a gentleman friend, Tony, a driving instructor who used the bungalow as a base for his driving school business. A slimy, creepy individual who everyone knew, except Tigger's mother, that he was only after one thing and that was her money. Tigger went out with Tony's sister for a while and she confirmed Tigger's suspicions.

174

"Tony only wants to be friends with your mother, like all the other old ladies he has befriended and get her to leave the bungalow to him in her will."

Just as Tigger had suspected!

Tigger confronted his mother one day about this. She went into a rage and told Tigger it was nothing of the sort, that Tony was a lovely man who would do anything for her. Tigger did not mention it again, at least for a while.

Tigger had to get into proper employment. He had very little money, he had nothing in the way of furniture or any real roots. He was-as said- at the bottom rung of the ladder. Reluctantly he applied for a job at the DHSS as a clerical clerk, after an eternal wait he was invited for an interview, something he had not experienced for years but managed to get through it and then after a further delay of a few weeks he received a letter offering him the position of clerical clerk starting at the Worthing Office. This was the first rung of the ladder that Tigger was about to crawl up! It was a strange feeling for Tigger being in an office again after so many years away from banking. But he stuck at it. He did not particularly like the work but it was a job, the pay was abysmal but maybe it would be a lever to getting something better later. His work colleagues were a mixed bunch but a few were good company. One was a girl he had known when he started banking, Angie. She had worked in the local opticians at the time, now married with a couple of boys. There were no ladies that were eligible, so no chance of meeting anyone at the DHSS. The job was very depressing and Tigger hated the benefits system where many who were in need, fell short and the others who knew how to work the system. He had to get out!!! But it was not going to be easy and would take some time.

In life sometimes there are moments that are destined to change one's life and so it was to be with Tigger. A phone call one evening from one of his ex-milk round customers, Val, with whom he had kept in touch with, was indeed set to change his life. It was soon to be her birthday and she was going to have a party at a local hotel in Littlehampton and she would be delighted if he would come.

"There is someone who is also coming with whom I think you will get along with just fine."

And so it was to be. A number of people there were familiar to Tigger but a lady called Wendy was a complete stranger. They were duly introduced to each other by Val. Now Wendy was recently separated from her husband and being rather nervous kept going to the loo and on one occasion Tigger passed a comment.

"I know a good plumber."

What a chat up line!

At the end of the evening Tigger was asked if he would give Wendy a lift home. They exchanged phone numbers but Tigger thought that would be it. *Wendy was a nice person*, he thought, but was not really interested in a long term relationship.

At the Coach and Horses one evening the pub phone rang, it was Val.

"Have you rung Wendy yet? She was expecting a call from you!!!"

After a day or so Tigger rang Wendy and they arranged a date.

They went to a lovely country pub near Arundel, The George and Dragon. Whilst Wendy sat down Tigger went to the bar to get drinks and when he returned Wendy was nowhere to be seen. It was rather a Dell Boy moment!!! Wendy being shy and nervous as if someone she knew may see her, she had taken herself off to a quiet Nook in the bar. They laughed about it and had a good evening.

That was the start of a long and happy relationship that is still going strong today.

Wen, as she was to be known from now on, introduced Tigger to her two boys, Ian and Keith and her mother, a lovely lady with whom Tigger always had a good relationship with. She never had a bad word to say about anyone.

The relationship that Tigger and Wen had grew stronger until they knew they were in love. Wen was to be the love of his life till the end of his days. Her ex-husband was living and working away in Cheltenham by now and eventually both Tigger and Wen had their respective divorces. Tigger got on very well with Ian and Keith, often taking them to football to see Brighton and Hove Albion, and they had good laughs together.

Tigger was getting absolutely zero satisfaction from his DHSS job and put in for promotion to the inland revenue, which Tigger's manager felt confident he would get. After several weeks he found out he was unsuccessful. It was the turning point for Tigger and he was determined, even more, to better himself. That failure to get the inland revenue job was the spur he needed to get himself out of the rut. In the meanwhile Tigger had moved in with Wen and a wedding was arranged.

Tigger's mother of course was invited. She even tried to put a spanner in the works with that! She seemed to get on well with Wen, which pleased everyone. However, his mother wanted Tony to be invited to the wedding, which both Tigger and Wen were adamant he would not! Of course a row was the result. It was pointed out to Tigger's mother that they wanted people at the wedding who were their friends and Tony certainly was not. They did not tell her they thought Tony was a greasy, slimy git who would be the last person they would invite. Mother threw tantrums, she was not coming etc. They let her calm down and eventually, as expected she went to the wedding at the local Registry Office, with the reception at a lovely old local restaurant, The Old Forge. Tigger's godfather attended along with a group of close friends including Ethel, his mother's neighbour and it proved to be a lovely occasion.

Wen with Ian and Keith as youngsters

After the west country honeymoon and back home all together in what was Wen's house, a big party was organised and many of Tigger's DHSS colleagues came and it was a really good time.

The new formed family all got used to being together and living happily. Ian and Keith were so good. The next target was for Tigger to find this new job.

It was Easter and Tigger had some time off.

"Wen, I am going to find another job."

"What do you fancy doing, then?"

"Estate Agency and I am going to take myself off round the village to all the agents to see if they need anyone."

One of the agents in Rustington where they lived was Whittaker and Co, owned by Derek Whittaker who Tigger knew years ago when he was in Young Conservatives.

Luckily Derek was there and remembered Tigger.

"I wonder whether you have any vacancies for a negotiator, and if so, whether you would consider me. I am currently working at the DHSS and the job is killing me with boredom!!!"

"What experience have you got?"

"None but I am very willing to give it a go if you could give me a chance."

"Well, you may be in luck. I am looking for someone in my Littlehampton Office for Saturday afternoons and Sunday mornings. You do not know whether you would like Estate Agency and I do not know whether I could work with you, is that a fair statement?"

"Yes I agree."

"Well, I am prepared to give you a chance, if you are willing to start with that arrangement and then if things work out and an opportunity arises, we can talk again."

Elated, Tigger returned home to tell Wen the good news. Could this be the start of something great?

The weeks went by working at The DHSS during the week but really looking forward to the weekend job at the Littlehampton Office. He took to Estate Agency like a duck to water and was soon selling property.

One day Tigger received a phone call from an old girl friend from his banking days, asking him if he would like to be in a play she was helping to put on. Tigger had taken part in the DHSS Amateur Dramatic Festival which he had enjoyed, so he agreed to go to the auditions and got a part in *Happiest Days of Your Life*. He enjoyed the time there, which spurred him on to joining Littlehampton Amateur Dramatic Society – LADS. He ended up taking part in several plays getting good reviews in the local Littlehampton Gazette. It was fun and the members were all good people.

One play, *Outside Edge* based on the successful TV series was a particular success and very funny. One of the actors had a part in which he was late for cricket practice and his line was,

"Sorry I am late I have been mowing the lawn and mending the fence."

During the first night performance these lines came out as,

"Sorry I am late I have been mending the lawn and mowing the fence."

It received such a laugh from the audience it was decided to leave the mistaken lines in!

Wen and Tigger were really enjoying their married life and one day after Tigger returned home from work Wen sat Tigger down.

"I have some potentially wonderful news for you. I have always thought how sad it was that you never had children. So, I have been to the doctor as I have been feeling so well over the last months and my Crohns Disease has not been affecting me. The doctor sees no reason why I should not try and get pregnant! What do you think?"

"I am speechless, of course I would love us to have a baby, but on my wage how can we afford it?"

"We will find a way."

"OK, let's go for it!!!"

After a few months Tigger had a phone call at work, something that rarely happened. It was Wen to tell him she was pregnant.

He jumped up and down with joy and his colleagues shared his delight. Well that was the first bit of wonderful news that year.

It was coming up to Christmas and a few office parties were being arranged, it was a Friday afternoon and they were all winding down ready to break for the weekend.

"Tigger there's a phone call for you, someone called Derek Whittaker?"

A phone call that was to yet again change his life.

"Hello, Tigger. Happy Christmas. I have some news that I hope will be an excellent Christmas present for you. I have an opening at my Rustington Office for you if you want to take it. I like what you have been doing at my Littlehampton Office over these last few months at the weekends."

"Thanks, Derek, you bet."

"Come in and see me in the next few days before Christmas and we can have a chat about pay and when you can start."

Well, talk about the best Christmas present for years, he could not wait to tell Wen and his line manager at the DHSS.

Chapter 28
Another New Chapter

After a very happy Christmas and even one Tigger's mother shared in his happiness, at the start of another new year Tigger found himself walking, with a great spring in his step, down the road to Rustington Village centre and into a new job. His own desk, his own name plate, a good pay rise and a company car. Could life get any better? Roger was the office manager, a man with a dry sense of humour who he had become acquainted with during his part time job at weekends. They soon built up a good, if competitive, working relationship. The property market was good and it was not long before Tigger tied up his first deal. Elated he punched the air.

"Well done, Tigger," remarked Derek Whittaker. "But remember, one swallow does not make a summer, just go out and sell another."

Which he did again and again and again. Even at weekends working in his garden Tigger would receive a phone call from a client wanting to view a property and ended up selling it!!!

After a short while, as Tigger was doing so well Derek gave him a pay rise and a higher commission rate. At last he and Wen could start saving some money. Wen worked at the local community hospital, which she loved, as an occupational therapist.

Wen's pregnancy was going very well, it was well into summer and Wen gave up work in preparation for the birth of their son. He was a very active baby in the womb and Wen was admitted to Chichester Hospital early as there was a minor problem so the medical team needed to keep an eye on her. It was a long, hot summer and come the 26th July it was evident there was not long to go! England were playing a test in cricket and it was the Olympics, so Tigger was rushing from Wen's bedside to the TV room, not wishing to miss out on either events!!! Then on the evening of the 27th Andrew Michael was born, 8lbs 12ozs. A near perfect birth and all was well. At last Tigger had a BLOOD relation he could call his own. He was a lovely baby!!!

The next day the boys, Tigger's mother and Wen's mother all went to see Wen and Andrew. The usual photo shoots taken. It was a really happy time.

In no time at all Wen and Andrew were home, it was 1984, certainly a year to remember. Life was certainly on the up once more.

Having gone through a relatively good period with his mother it was not long before Tigger's mother started her tantrums again. She was delighted at having her first and only grandchild, the question of names came up. They all knew it was going to be Andrew long before the birth, but as to any other names, well that had not been decided.

"Of course he has to have Bernard in his name. I insist upon that!"

Well neither Tigger or Wen took too kindly to being TOLD what they should have as Andrew's other names. They

184

wanted Michael but had not considered a third name and they told Tigger's mother that.

"Well I will cut you out of my will if you do not include Bernard."

Well the knives certainly seemed to be out. The rows continued. It was not the fact that Bernard had been suggested as a further name but the manner in which Tigger's mother had asked or rather told them what they should call their new baby.

"I will give you 500 pounds if you call him Bernard."

Well they certainly were not going to be blackmailed into submitting to her demands.

However after things calmed down somewhat and Tigger and Wen spoke about it they reluctantly decided that in memory of Tigger's Dad it would be good if Andrew had a third name, Bernard but it only need be used in official forms etc. So he was to be Andrew Michael BERNARD!!!

Needless to say the 500 pounds never appeared, not that that worried Tigger or Wen.

The months passed, the first Christmas with Andrew, Keith and Ian – a lovely time.

April was fast approaching and Tigger's birthday, how nice it would be for Tigger and Wen to go out together by themselves for the first time since Andrew's birth. The boys volunteered to baby sit and if there were any problems Tigger and Wen would only be close by at a local pub. Off they went to enjoy a pleasant evening. After a couple of drinks Tigger suggested they went somewhere else, maybe for a meal. Wen was happy to stay where they were and have just one more drink. The barmaid was a friend of Wen and came over to say a message had been received from the boys back home that

Andrew was screaming the house down and they did not know what to do. Hot footing it back to the house, they noticed Andrew's bedroom light was not on. Strange! Tigger was not best pleased and asked what the matter with Andrew was.

"Oh, he seems to be OK now and has settled down."

A disgruntled Tigger opened the lounge door to find it full of their friends and neighbours.

"What the hell are you lot doing here?" asked Tigger.

"HAPPY BIRTHDAY! Surprise, Surprise!"

Tigger had never had a surprise party before. Wen and friends had organised it all without raising any suspicions with Tigger. Food had been hidden under beds and with neighbours.

An ordinary birthday had turned out to be a wonderful occasion with good friends and neighbours!!! Tigger felt very touched. Wen should have done this for him.

Tigger was continuing to do well at Whittaker's and life with Wen and Andrew was great.

Tigger's mother was up and down with her moods. She was, by this time, very close to Tony the driving instructor. He had a key to her bungalow, he spent every lunch time with her.

Tigger's mother had also built up a good friendship with Ethel, her neighbour. Ethel had been an eye specialist during her working life in London, where her husband, Professor Kenneth Franklin was also specialising at Guys Hospital. They were obviously very well off. They had one daughter who lived in Canada. They were a good family way out of Tigger's mother's league but she managed to find her way into Ethel's affections.

Kenneth had died some years previously and Ethel was by herself. Tigger's mother had been a good friend, having Ethel every Sunday for lunch and then watching TV together until the late evening. Tigger felt, like Tony, his mother also had an ulterior motive for her close friendship with Ethel, money. Tony could see that both Tigger's mother and Ethel had money. And so the tangled web was formed. Tony was well in, as it were, by now with both old ladies, taking them out for Sunday lunch at top country pubs or restaurants and then later on to holidays to Scotland and then to Switzerland. How odd that a man in his 50s would find pleasure in taking two old ladies on holiday!!!

Whenever he and Tigger met there was a very uneasy politeness. Tigger was itching to give him a piece of his mind, but he would bide his time, his time WOULD come!

During Tigger's time at the office in Rustington he became acquainted with quite a number of people. Some were little old ladies who just wanted to pass the time having a chat. One such lady who came into the office during a lull in business and chatted to both Tigger and Roger. She lived in a small block of flats nearby, mostly retired ladies.

Mrs Oram was a lovely old dear and chatted away.

"Yes it does get a bit lonely by yourself in the flat. We sometimes have get togethers, but I have no relatives to come and see me. The lady downstairs, now she is lucky, she has this nice driving instructor chap who regularly visits her and takes her shopping."

"Oh that's nice, his name is not Tony by any chance is it?" Tigger asked.

"Oh yes, it is. Do you know him then?"

"Yes I am acquainted with him."

"Nice chap, and so charming."

Tigger was 99% sure it was Tony, how could it be anyone else? But he wanted to make sure. Then one day his luck was in, driving past the old ladies block of flats, whose car was parked outside? Of course, the car belonging to Tony.

Evidence was building up, but a long way to go.

Rustington was a close knit community and the houses just up from Tigger's office also had a lot of retired folk living there. On yet another day driving up there for a viewing with a client, lo and behold there was Tony's car parked outside the house of yet another retired lady. His car was still parked outside on his return to the office.

One Sunday on his weekly visit to his mother to mow the lawn and tend to her garden, Tigger could not believe his eyes when whose car was in front of him. Yes, Tony the driving instructor. Tigger followed at a distance and yes, he was visiting his old lady friend in the block of flats off of Sea Lane.

Tigger did not mention this to his mother for a while, preferring to take his time and choose his moment. Tony, incidentally lived over in Brighton, so there was no need for him to be in Rustington at the weekends.

The following weekend, when Tigger's mother was praising Tony for being so good to her, oh yes, she knew how to play Tony against Tigger. Tigger thought that now was the time to let a few little Tony secrets out.

"Did Tony come over and see you last weekend, by any chance, Mother?"

"No Tony never comes here at weekends. He has far too much to do at his home and meet up with his partner and spend time with him. Why?"

"Oh I thought I saw him going down Sea Lane and drive into the entrance of Rowan Court, a block of flats."

"Good gracious no. And anyway Tony would never have come over and not come to see me, you are mistaken."

"Oh I do not think so, but never mind."

The next week, Tigger could see by the look of thunder on his mother's face that all was not well. An expression he had seen many many times before.

"You are trying to drive a wedge between Tony and me. Tony was nowhere near here last weekend. He was at home in Brighton. You are evil, why can you not leave me to be friends with Tony, he has done nothing to you?"

Time went by and Andrew was growing up fast. Ian and Keith acted like blood brothers to him and they all got on so well. Andrew had started pre-school, first at Holmes Lane Rustington and then later at one at East Preston where Wen now worked.

Tigger and Andrew were expected to visit his mother every Sunday without fail to tend to her garden but when Tigger and the family wanted to go out for the day and he would then miss a Sunday, then the tantrums started.

"Oh well, of course, if you have no time to spend with your mother and you need to go out with your family, I will have to find someone else to do my garden. Perhaps, Tony will know of someone."

She certainly knew the buttons to press! Bloody Tony always came into the equation!!!

Tigger used to love spending Sunday evenings chilling out with his lovely family, so he was ready for the new working week. Quite often Tigger's mother would ring up.

"My TV is not working and it is my favourite programme. Can you come over and see what's wrong?"

Invariably the TV just needed the mains plug or the TV aerial to be connected. Then she would expect Tigger to stay.

"You are not going now you are here? I never see anyone."

It was a sad way to try and manipulate Tigger but he had his own family and his mother saw Tony every weekday and Tigger and Andrew at weekends and Ethel came for tea. So, never see anyone?

As time went on Ethel went to live in a local old peoples home and Tigger had to ferry her back and forth on a Sunday. It was evident that Tigger's mother was thinking that Ethel was getting older and the time would come that she would pass on. She started to work on Ethel on the Sunday visits.

"Your daughter never comes over to see you at all and I know you two did not always get on. You should leave your money to those who have looked after you."

Tigger was witness to what his mother said as he was there to take Ethel back to the home.

He was shocked his mother should be saying such things. But it soon made him realise what she was up to. Ethel was often in tears in Tigger's car on the way back to the home.

"Your mother is good to me but she has a sharp tongue sometimes and I do not know what I have done."

"Nothing, Ethel, you should know my mother well enough now to know what she can be like."

Rthelwas a lovely lady and did not have a bad word to say about anyone. So sad she was being manipulated in this way.

Sometime later Tigger found out that his mother and Ethel paid a visit to Ethel's solicitor and Ethel's will was changed, to what, Tigger was unaware, but he had his suspicions. His mother had obviously worked on Ethel enough then.

Chapter 29
A Holiday Abroad

Tigger's mother had the habit of changing like the wind. On many occasions Tigger dreaded his Sunday visits as did Andrew but on one occasion she produced a cheque for one thousand pounds.

"I do not want you telling people you do the garden for nothing so here is a cheque – book up a holiday to Switzerland. Of course had you kept in touch with Aunt Evelyn you would have inherited her thousands when she died, then you would not have had to rely on me for money."

Aunt Evelyn was indeed a very wealthy person and he was sad to have lost touch with them because of his mother but sometimes happiness and well-being is more important than money!

The wind was taken out of Tigger's sails. He thanked his mother very much and could not wait to get back home to tell Wen. She had always wanted to go to Switzerland as Tigger had told her so much about it, having spent a few holidays there with his parents.

A wonderful spring time holiday was spent in a small village just outside Interlaken in the Bernese Oberland area of Switzerland Wildersvil. They had flown to Zurich and then taken a train from there via Berne to Interlaken. The journey was indeed wonderful spring mountain flowers, trips up the highest mountains, travelling through the mighty Eiger mountain tunnel and on up to the Jungfrau and seeing wonderful ice carvings deep in the mountain glacier. Trips on the two large lakes, Thun and Brienz, seeing magnificent waterfalls tumbling into the lake. Andrew loved the holiday as well taking in all the beautiful scenery. Wen had never travelled abroad before so it was a wonderful experience for her as well. Many photos taken so they could reminisce for years to come.

On returning home to work Tigger and Roger were aware that Derek Whitaker was having meetings in the upstairs office on several occasions with the same man. Something was afoot! It was a time when insurance companies and building societies were taking over groups of estate agents – Derek had five offices by now. Suspicions were confirmed.

Then came the day when Derek ushered all the staff to the upstairs meeting room.

"First of all I want to thank Roger and Tigger for their discretion. You will have been aware of the many meetings I have been having with a certain gentleman over the past few weeks, and yet you kept your council and no rumours went around.

"I have some bad news and some very good news. The bad news is that I have sold my business to the Prudential Insurance Company and we are no longer Derek Whitaker Estate Agency.

"The very good news is that I shall become your area director, all your jobs are secure and I have negotiated very good pay rises for you all. Roger and Tigger, you will both have new company cars of your choice. I will be having private talks with all of you to go through your new contracts. Any questions? If not back to work and show your new paymasters what we can do."

There were various changes over the weeks and months to come. Tigger and Roger both chose new Rover cars. Tigger had to go to several meetings in Guildford to organise new for sale boards and do returns of the number of boards in the area Derek was in control of.

Roger always joked that Tigger was going to a board meeting.

Tigger was performing so well that other agents in the area were becoming aware of his successes, so much so that he was head hunted by a rival agent. Roger pleaded with Tigger not to go, he said he would be leaving Whitakers soon, he had enough and Tigger would be manager then. Roger was a little cavalier at times with his comments and Tigger did not take Roger's word and so it was with great reluctance that he decided to take the offer from Pascoe and Partners. He was to become manager of one of their local offices. Derek was disappointed but pointed out that if Tigger ever wanted to return, just pick up the phone.

The manager's job at Pascoe and Partners was certainly a step up. The office was in a quieter part of the area. Tigger had two staff, Alistair and Corrine, much younger than him but they all got on well and Alistair was very much a character. Richard Pascoe was the principal partner and based himself at Angmering where Tigger was based also. Richard was a very tall heavily built man, but with a gentle disposition.

One day one of the local property developers, John Lower, came into the office for one of his regular chats and put a large, rusty lump of metal on his desk.

"What the heck is that?" exclaimed Tigger.

"Remember you used to live at No 13 Arundel Road Castle Goring? Well, I have bought the whole site. The stables have gone and Mary, your ex, has re married and lives in Wales. I am going to re develop the whole area into high class homes and have started on No 13 first. The lads found this at the cottage!"

"What is it?" asked Tigger.

"It's the detonator from a German World War II bomb!"

Tigger knew a bomber had reportedly dumped its bombs in the area on its dash back to Germany.

"So it could have gone up at any time with you living there!!!"

"Sorry don't think so!"

Tigger started to get on well in his new role but was soon aware that Richard was having meetings with 'men in suits' on a regular basis, sometimes with the other partners. Tigger, Alistair and Corrine were all beginning to get suspicious something was going on and Tigger had seen this before at Whittakers. A bit of déjà vu. It was not long before their suspicions became founded. A meeting of all staff from Pascoe's other offices. Yes, another buy out by a building society. Nothing much would change, they were told apart from rebranding nothing would change and no hefty pay rise either this time. There was a degree of unease amongst many of the staff including Tigger.

After a while things settled down again. At the time there was the beginnings of a UK recession and the housing market was also affected. Pressures started to build and although Tigger and his team were selling reasonably well, it was not always to the satisfaction of Richard Pascoe, who by now was a regional director of the new company. He was a good man to work with but now, as a regional director there were additional pressures being put upon him that were not there under the original partnership!

Tigger was keeping in regular contact with Derek Whittaker. The atmosphere was now certainly not as good as it had been at Whittakers. Tigger could see the distinct possibility of his office being closed down, so he decided to act before things turned nasty. After a couple of meetings with Derek, Tigger found himself back working for Derek at the Worthing office, temporary, he was told until the then manager at Rustington was gone!!! Derek had got Tigger earmarked for the Rustington Office as the manager and Derek there was not seeing eye to eye.

Back at Rustington Tigger felt more at home as he was, once again, under the "wing" of Derek. He and Derek got on well. Derek always kept Tigger informed what was going on in the company. Sales were good, for a while. The recession was beginning to bite and once again the pressures to sell were being felt. Derek was from the old school and knew these things happened from time to time, ride out the storm and things would eventually come good but companies do not always think like that and they wanted results NOW!!!

One day Tigger received a call from Derek. He was summoned to go over to Worthing to see Derek. Walking into his office he felt something was wrong. There were a few boxes around and Derek was putting his personal belongings into these boxes.

"Hi, thanks for coming over. I wanted to speak to you personally rather than over the phone. I am leaving and wanted you to be the first to know."

Shocked, Tigger asked why.

"Well, as you know by now, I have not been getting on that well with one of the directors. We have been having a series of heated discussions. I have not been happy with the way he is running things, so in the end I have decided I cannot work with someone like that.

"Keep your head down and do the best you can. Things have changed and not for the better, in my opinion and I do not think it will stop, so be very wary."

Tigger expressed his disappointment and asked what Derek would do now. Obviously, Derek, had a big pay-out when he sold his business, so he had a few options in starting up another business.

It was with a heavy heart that Tigger returned to his Rustington office to tell his staff. Corrine had by this time left Pascoe and joined Tigger at Rustington. They were all a little subdued but Tigger soon sparked them into action. They had a job to do, because if they did not get on with it then THEIR jobs would be in jeopardy also.

Home life continued to be good. Andrew was fast growing and developing his own strong character and was beginning to 'test the boundaries' as all children do. He was doing quite well at his little pre-school. It was getting to the stage when Tigger and Wen were thinking about sending him to primary school locally until on one of Tigger's Sunday visits to his mother, she suddenly came out with,

"I would like to send Andrew to private school. You had a private education and it did you good. I will pay for the fees.

A couple of years at Firth House will do him the world of good. He will meet some nice boys there."

Shocked, surprised and a little suspicious, Tigger reported back to Wen. They talked things over and again with Mother. A meeting with the Head of Firth House, was followed by buying the new school uniform and Andrew visiting the school prior to the new term. Firth House was in Rustington, so very convenient. It was agreed that Andrew would go to Firth House for the two years Mother had suggested. The new term was soon upon them and Andrew started at his new school and was soon enjoying lessons and making new friends.

All this was very good but Tigger and Wen knew that now Mother had a tighter control on them.

Tigger had a company car, and Wen also had a car, a battered old black Mini , fast reaching the end of its days until one day, the driver's door fell off!!! It was, to say the least, a rust bucket.

Now Wen used to take Tigger's mother for her weekly shop, and upon learning the Mini was going to its grave, quickly announced that Wen must have another car otherwise she cannot take me shopping. A small second hand Honda was found, purchased by Mother and all was well for now!!!

Time went on and Tigger's mother became more demanding as to when she wanted to be taken out, not only for the weekly shop but on other shopping trips and for doctors' appointments. Wen worked and had Andrew and the other two boys to think of and care for, so it was not always convenient to drop everything to go on a shopping trip with Mother. Wen also had her own mother living locally to visit and keep an eye on. The atmosphere was becoming more and more frosty. Wen was reminded in no uncertain terms that although Wen had the car it was really HER car and it was not unreasonable to want to be taken around in the car when SHE wanted. The screw was gradually being turned until Wen was late one day for the weekly shopping trip and upon arriving at Mother's a big row erupted. Shopping was done in silence and Wen returned home in tears. When Tigger got home, Wen was still upset. Things could not carry on like this and she was not going to be subjected to being blackmailed by Tigger's mother.

The next day Wen went with a friend and the car was taken back to Tigger's mother with a note to say the car was being returned and she was not going to be spoken to like that again. They managed to get the car in the driveway, drive away in the friends car without having to confront Mother.

The expected phone call from Mother raging on never arrived!!! With some reluctance Tigger went round for his usual weekend visit expecting the worst but was met with virtual silence. Tigger refused to be drawn into an argument, so never mentioned the car episode either. He did what he had to in the garden and returned home. As time went on relations began to improve once again but the treading on eggshells atmosphere remained. There seemed to be an uneasy truce. Ethel would be taken to and from Mother's on a Sunday and life went on.

Tigger had been increasingly wanting to find out about his natural born parents and had made one or two failed attempts to trace his mother and father. Tigger and Wen had decided to take a trip to London and to the Records Office. A fascinating building with rooms full of records of births, marriages, deaths and adoptions. But where to start? There were large books dating back to the times of handwritten records with quill pens and up to the present day. Tigger had always been of the opinion, he did not know why, that his parents either married just before World War II or just after, when Tigger was born. He decided to go for the former, and low and behold after flicking through a couple of pages, there it was, his birth parents marriage certificate. From all of the record books he could have chosen the first one he chose provided him with an opening!!! He wrote down all the information, so that he could apply for a copy of the marriage certificate. Job done, he could get so much more information from sites on his computer at home – so he thought! They would leave and have a browse around London whilst they were up there. Just before leaving Wen asked Tigger,

"Would you not like to see the records for your adoption?"

Eventually they found the record and with some interesting information. Andrew was born on the 27th July and what was the date Tigger was formally adopted. 27th July 1949!!! What a coincidence. All in all the days visit and experience had been a lot to take in and quite an emotional one.

Upon returning home, Tigger set about trying to find out more information about his parents. He started with his father. He knew his date of birth, that he was a career soldier in the RAMC – Royal Army Medical Corp. Tigger's grandfather had been a pharmacist in the Cotswolds, so maybe a natural path to take for his father. He went into the Army at 18 and progressed through the ranks to sergeant. He obviously wanted to further his Army career but as a Commissioned Officer not as an NCO. So he had to leave the Army, a technicality and re-join, having applied for a 2nd Lieutenant.

He progressed to Major and Camp Commandant at Colchester barracks – still in the RAMC. Tigger applied to Army Records for more information but all they would tell Tigger was his date of death in 1986. *Oh well to be expected,* thought Tigger, but at least he had the date of death and that could open up more doors, again, so he thought. That was to prove a sticking point for now. Searching various sites, using his father's name and an alias he apparently used during the war (Tigger was never to find the reason for this) he even thought he may have been a secret agent! He always came to a dead end. NO RECORD FOUND!!! The mystery surrounding his father continued a while longer.

It was one Sunday when Wen was at church and Tigger had not gone to his mother's for his usual Sunday visit. He was tending his own garden. It was a time when he could think and cast his mind back to his early days. He recalled his Sunday school visits to the local Christian Science Church just around the corner and on an impulse he decided to take himself off to the church to see if anyone remembered the Stuart Whittons. On arriving at the church a group of ladies were putting away the hymn and prayer books. One particularly elderly lady looked up at Tigger and asked if she could help.

"It may seem a strange question, but I wonder if there is anyone here who remembers a family attending this church many years ago, named Stuart Whitton, a long shot I know."

"Oh yes I remember them well and you must be Tigger?"

A shiver went through Tigger, astounded that after nearly 50 years, he was standing in front of someone who remembered him after all this time and recognised it was him!!!

"I remember you well as a little boy, the Stuart Whittons were a nice family, they had a daughter, but I have no idea what happened to the daughter after her parents died, so sorry I cannot be of any more help but nice to see you, and good luck with your endeavours."

Tigger returned home and told Wen what had happened and thought it remarkable that someone living on their doorstep still recalled the Sunday church visits Tigger had made as a small child with the Stuart Whittons.

Chapter 30
The Years Go By

Family life was good. Andrew was growing up fast and was a member of the local cub scout group and Wen a leader. There were some very amusing times as Keith was maturing and he spent a lot of time down in his shed, painting what to the family were weird and wonderful paintings – skulls featured heavily and little books of writings of his private thoughts. He and Ian were good lads and thought the world of their mother and they had by now fully accepted Tigger into the family. Tigger though had to them a most peculiar upbringing and they had no warmth towards Tigger's mother. They very occasionally were persuaded to visit Tigger's mother and they did some weeding in her garden for which she said she would pay them for a whole mornings work, a measly 20p, needless to say they stopped going round to see her, they called her E.T.!!!

Keith was increasingly turning into a Goth and one day on returning from his work Tigger was met by a sniggering Ian and Wen!!! What was going on?

"You had better prepare yourself for a bit of a shock."

And more laughing.

Keith appeared, having had a complete makeover!!! His hair was dyed black and fully spiked up! And a complete black set of clothes!!!

"What the hell have you done?" Tigger exclaimed.

"Chill out," Ian said, "and get over it."

Keith was well into the cure and way out music so his new image fitted perfectly!!!

After a while with Keith's new image Andrew was developing a cough which the doctor was unable to diagnose. Then one day when Keith was out Tigger and Ian had a rummage through Keith's bedroom and found 15 empty cans of hairspray dotted around various hiding places. That was the reason for Andrews cough!!! The spray floating around the house was causing the cough. A few choice words to Keith and apologies, found him spraying his hair down the bottom of the garden!!!

Soon Ian had left school and was working at the Norfolk Hotel in Arundel. Keith, who had a more academic brain, was working hard at school and knew exactly what he wanted to do. Tigger's mother was up and down with her moods and Ethel had increasingly poor health.

Further holidays in Switzerland to Wildersvil were enjoyed and made a welcome break from the stresses of work and Tigger's mother.

A phone call one day from Tigger's mother with the news that poor Ethel had passed away.

The funeral came and went and then the inevitable clearing of her apartment she still had. Furniture, painting etc. Being quite wealthy she had a few valuable possessions and of course Tony helped himself to some good pieces of furniture. Tigger had a couple of nice original oil paintings of old sailing galleons. His mother inherited the lion's share of Ethel's estate amounting to many many thousands. Ethel's daughter had a bequest enough to prevent a challenge to the will! Tigger's mother was besotted with money but spent very little. Tigger and Wen were very sad at the loss of Ethel as she was such a lovely lady and were sorry that, at times, Tigger's mother had treated Ethel so badly.

It was the late 1980s and the UK recession continued. The property market began to be affected and pressures began to mount for Tigger. He had to work longer hours. His team had to spend hours phoning clients and trying to get more sales. It was getting more and more difficult and he was unhappy at the rather unprofessional tactics his company was asking him and other managers to make, such as trying to take properties from their competitors. In the days of Derek Whitaker and Richard Pascoe respect for competitors was observed and such tactics were rarely heard of. Tigger was increasingly uneasy with his job and employers. His mother was going through one of her particularly unpleasant episodes, picking and moaning about everything.

Things were beginning to come to a head at work and Tigger continued to feel increasingly uneasy. The area manager was putting more and more pressure on him to sell, encouraging the falsifying of the weekly figures so that he would qualify for a new car if a certain number of sales were achieved from the area. Tigger wanted no part in that. Christmas was fast approaching and a short welcome break. It gave him time to think.

New Year arrived and more and more pressure. Tigger was nearly at breaking point. Meetings were held making it known that more sales had to be achieved and jobs would be on the line for those that failed. One morning Tigger arrived at his office and told his staff that he could not put up with it any longer and could not work under such unfair conditions or pressures, he was resigning. Car keys on his desk with office keys and then goodbye.

Arriving home Wen was surprised to see him and asked if he was ill.

"No, I have resigned. I now have no job."

"What the hell are we going to do without your money coming in?"

"Something will happen, of that I am convinced. We have some savings that will last us a few months. I just could not carry on working for that shower, under so much pressure and asking me to do things which were really wrong. I would be committing fraud and I want no part in that. Estate Agency is a profession and what they are encouraging the guys to do is certainly not professional."

As they say, one door closes and another opens. Tigger really believed that.

In order to prevent further problems and hassle Tigger did not tell his mother that he had walked out of his job.

The days and weeks passed. Tigger had to sign on at the Employment Office in order to collect any benefits he was due. Not much compared with what he had been earning. He hated having to do that but every penny counted now. Tigger busied himself looking for work and redecorating the house. He felt very low and he knew it was a worry to Wen but she was so supportive of Tigger and they never rowed about him being out of work but he felt positive that something would change and for the better. He was not sure what he wanted to do. Whether he wanted to remain in an estate agency, or not!!!

An ex colleague of his who was with him in estate agency who had been the manager in the neighbouring town of Littlehampton, had left some time before and was working for an insurance and investment company, Friends Provident.

"Why don't you come and work for us?" he said.

"They are looking to recruit big time as they are starting a new sales division."

"Oh I do not want to go door to door trying to get business. I do not think that is for me."

"It's not at all like that, you receive proper training and they give you an area to work to and loads of existing clients-you do not have to go knocking on doors for business."

So the long journey of applying for this job started. His good friend, Mick, helped Tigger to write his CV in a most professional way and a letter was sent to the local Friends Provident Office in Horsham applying for the position of financial advisor.

After five rather gruelling interviews including role plays and interviews, the area director commented,

"Do you not think you are a little old for this job?"

To which Tigger replied,

"Age is a number and grey is the colour of my hair, what's your next question?"

They even interviewed Wen, to make sure she was fully aware of what the job involved and the long hours he would have to work in the early days. Tigger was aged 48 and to change jobs which involved taking many exams and hours of training was a very daunting challenge but one he felt obliged he would have to take. It was like the last chance saloon!!! After the final interview it was only a matter of a day or two before he had a telephone call confirming his appointment followed by an official letter. YES!!! Tigger was up and running again, much to the relief of both Tigger and Wen.

Chapter 31
The End of an Era

The whole family was relieved that Tigger was again earning money, into a new job and a new experience. Keith had, by this time, finished with his A-Levels and with excellent passes. So university beckoned. But which one, obviously an art school/university and so it was to be, Wimbledon School of Art, part of Guildford University. Grants were successfully made and so Keith left home and embarked on his new life. Meanwhile Tigger had started at the Horsham office and hit the ground running with CBT, Computer Based Training. A couple of weeks learning the basics before a residential course at Salisbury Head Office, intensive training and exams, training and more exams!!! Back at Horsham and more in house training whilst Tigger references were checked out. Tigger had told his mother that he had changed jobs and was much happier now. She was very sceptical, Tigger was hoping that she would welcome and congratulate him on getting potentially such a good job. Unfortunately, their relationship again started to deteriorate, until one Sunday a big row erupted and Tigger stormed out telling his mother, 'The Worm Has Turned,' and that he would not continue to be spoken like that by her ever again. If she did not want to treat him as a son and welcome his Sunday visits then that would be the end. Tigger returned home shaking with rage, Wen was upset that Tigger was in such a state!!!

The weeks went by and Tigger never made any more Sunday visits. It was a sad situation, made worse. Soon after returning to work one Monday morning, the office manager called Tigger into the office.

"I have your references and it does not look good."

Tigger's heart sank.

"What's the problem?"

"You tell me. We have a problem with one of your previous employers, with an adverse reference. Maybe you can tell me about it."

"Well if you can tell me which employer maybe we can start a discussion about it."

"Oh, I cannot do that by reason of confidentiality."

"Is it my last employer?"

"Sorry, I cannot reveal that."

"Well, where do we go from here?"

"I am afraid we will have to terminate your contract. Have you your car keys and enough money for your train fare home?"

Tigger was distraught. He had NEVER been treated like this and never been sacked from a job ever in his life. He telephoned Wen with the news and asked her to meet him from the train station.

It was a bit like a game of snakes and ladders but it was no game. He was once again struggling to know what to do but once again Wen was so supportive and believed, like Tigger, that things would work out!

Having gathered his thoughts after a day or two he contacted his ex-colleague, Paul, who worked in the Friends Provident Portsmouth office. Tigger suspected the adverse reference was from his last job, the estate agents. He had maybe rather stupidly written to the CEO of the company to tell him how the local area manager had encouraged office managers to rig the weekly figures, this being the reason he had left. So when the area manager received Tigger's reference form he had responded appropriately!!!

Paul said it would not be a problem. He would get Tigger his job back. But as the weeks went by nothing happened. Things were becoming very strained at home with Tigger out of work once again. Where would they go from here? So one day Tigger grabbed the bull by the horns fed up with waiting for his friend at the Portsmouth Office to do something so he rang human resources at Friends Provident HQ at Dorking. Fortunately the woman he spoke to knew the CEO of the estate agents personally. The next day Tigger received a phone call from Dorking.

"Hi, I have some news which I am sure you will be relieved to hear. I have spoken to the CEO and he confirms that there is no problem with you and he endorses your references. You can re-join the Horsham Branch, or, if you wish, you can choose another local office. Good luck."

At last things were going his way and he could get back on track but he did not want to return to the Horsham Office as he felt the manager there gave him no support at all. With this in mind Tigger decided to ring the manager of the Portsmouth Office and arrange an interview with him. Bob Dowling was a no nonsense manager but welcomed Tigger on board but if he was to ever overstep the mark at any time he would be out of the door. Tigger obviously assured Bob he would work hard and be a credit to the office. They ended up lifelong pals. A phone call to Wen assured her all was well and he was back in employment again, but a lot of hard work lay ahead. However, the rewards could be life changing!

So it was to be and Tigger was reinstated at the Portsmouth Office and to yet more training and residential courses. He got on very well with all of his colleagues and had a good feeling about this job. They called him affectionately 'The Old Git'! He knew there was a lot of hard work to go through. At 48 he did not relish the idea of so much training and exams but if he was to succeed he would have to go through a certain amount of pain!!!

A phone call one weekend was from Tigger's mother's neighbour.

"I thought you ought to know that your mother is in hospital, she had a fall recently and was found on the hall floor."

The neighbours were fully aware how Tigger's mother had treated him and they had heard the many rows from their house!!! They knew of Tony and thought he was up to no good, an odd relationship, they thought and had their suspicions as to what he was up to.

Tigger felt obliged to visit his mother in hospital at Worthing. She seemed pleased to see him. He told her about his new job and that he was getting on well. She always spoke loudly and disturbed other patients with her voice. She had breathing problems, being an asthmatic. She did not seem unduly poorly but would have to stay in hospital a while as she lived by herself and the authorities had to make sure if she returned home she was capable of looking after herself.

On one hospital visit, Tigger could hear his mother in FULL voice talking to the 'lovely' Tony. Tigger did not wish to be in the company of Tony so remained around the corner at the reception desk.

"Have you come to see you mother then?" said the ward sister.

"Yes I have but she already has a visitor."

"Oh yes, Tony!!! We all know him well. He is always in here visiting all his old lady friends. We know what he is up to!!! I have also had to give him a warning. He keeps bringing in medication for your mother, inhalers, which we have caught her using far too much. We strictly administer your mother's medication and by having these inhalers only hinders any possible recovery. I have told Mr Tinkler if I catch him again he will be banned from the hospital."

Another confirmation of what Tony was up to with his mother, as if he needed it.

Having paid a short visit to his mother Tigger bade his farewells and left the hospital.

Along the rear of the hospital on the way to the car park, who should he bump into but Tony! With a smarmy grin Tony tried to engage in small talk. What an opportunity with no one in sight!!!

"Whilst I have you alone, Tony, I know just what you are up to with my mother and the many other old ladies you are friendly with. You are only after one thing, their money. The game is up, Tony, and I know about your visits to these old ladies in hospital as well, you are gaining quite a reputation."

The look on his face was a picture, the blood drained from his face!!! Tigger left quickly before Tony could make a reply.

That evening Tigger received a phone call from Tony threatening him with legal action. Tigger's response was,

"Go on, do it then. I will expect a letter from your solicitor?"

That was the last time Tigger ever had contact with Tony.

There were the usual, mandatory hospital visits over the next week or so. Tigger told his mother more about his new job and how well he was doing.

"Don't go spending your money on paying into pensions, when I go you will have my money."

This is something she had told Tigger on many occasions when they were on good terms but he was not convinced. She had also said on occasions that she did not like the idea of leaving her money to Tigger and then giving it to Ian and Keith.

"Don't go giving them the money, they are no relations of mine."

Tigger knew his mother by now had accumulated quite a small fortune in shares and building society deposits, plus the value of her bungalow. Of course Tony was aware of this as well!!!

"How long will my mother be in hospital, what are your plans for her?" Tigger asked the duty Sister.

"We are waiting for a bed to become available at Swandean Hospital and then we can open the champagne to celebrate her going, she really has been a pain and upset some of the other patients. We have also had to stop that Tony bringing in her inhalers for her again and have warned him again that should he continue do it we would ban him from visiting, we are suspicious as to why he keeps doing this."

Tigger's mother had numerous inhalers accumulated over time. How, he did not know and an overdose could prove dangerous if not fatal!!! Tony had kept taking them into the hospital against the hospital instructions. The hospital administered their own medication for Christine. Why was Tony bringing in these inhalers?

After a few days mother was transferred to Swandean, a hospital caring mainly for the elderly, an altogether smaller unit.

Tigger and Wen had booked a show at Brighton one Saturday and on their way dropped in to see his mother. She seemed agitated and was rambling on somewhat but not unduly unwell, they thought. Tigger and Wen had a good evening and returned home and were getting ready for bed when the phone rang.

"Good evening, I am sorry to ring you so late, but I have some sad news to tell you. Your mother passed away peacefully earlier on this evening."

TIGGER and Wen hugged each other. A sense of relief overwhelmed both of them. This was truly the end of an era.

The next few weeks and months were to be quite traumatic and life changing in many ways for Tigger and his family. Tigger told Andrew, Keith and Ian that there were no tears, only a feeling that life could be a little more relaxed and less stressful. BUT first there was the little matter of getting through the funeral and the relatives!!!

"Nana was not a very nice person, was she Mum and Dad?" Andrew commented.

"No maybe not but in her way she loved you very much."

"Huh, she had a very funny way of showing it sometimes."

Out of the mouths of babes, Andrew was aged ten by now and this would be the first funeral he would have to go to. We would all be there as a family supporting one another.

A visit to Swandean hospital to collect his mother's belongings was the first of a few 'Tony happenings'.

"I can give you the certificate for cause of death but Tony has collected your mothers belongings."

"Why did you do that? I am her son."

"Oh, he showed us he had power of attorney."

"WHAT?"

Tigger could do nothing about it but he was fuming. On the way back home, they called at the bungalow, only to find the locks had been changed on the doors. Tigger could not get in.

The neighbour confirmed that, in their opinion, Tony had had the locks changed.

Tony was certainly acting quickly to make sure Tigger was shut out.

On returning home, Tigger and Wen looked at the cause of death. Basically, severe respiratory tract problems. Hmm, those inhalers.

Tigger contacted his mother's relatives, cousins in Leicester to tell them the news. They already knew as Tony had already been in touch. Cousin Beatrice confirmed that Tony had changed the locks and that Tigger was not to go to the bungalow until she came down to sort his mother's belongings out. Tigger had never liked Beatrice and it was obvious Tony had sowed bad seeds about Tigger.

Tigger felt very tempted to go to the police to have Tony investigated about the inhalers and what the hospital had said, but thought better of it, preferring to wait until he had seen his mother's will. He and the family had been through enough, so could they all go through the trauma of a police investigation and all that would go with it?

The day of the funeral came at Worthing Crematorium. Tigger, Wen and Andrew were there, supported by neighbours, who knew exactly what his mother had been like and what Tigger had been through in his early life and latterly. Cousins from Leicester and Tony sat away from Tigger, even Tigger's mother's butcher was there! Why?

During the address by the minister he spoke of how Christine was a caring person, taking time to look after Ethel, her neighbour and good friend (oh yes so she would inherit Ethels fortune). But there was another side to Christine he remarked, one of greed for money and how badly she treated some members of her family. She had a Jekyll and Hyde character.

Tigger felt awful, he did not expect this and had not authorised the minster to say these things about his mother. He could have dug a hole!

After the ceremony as they were leaving the Crematorium Tigger told the minister he was not happy with what he had said.

"I could not be a hypocrite knowing how she had treated your family and experiencing Wen in tears many times in my office."

The Cousins would not speak much to Tigger only to say, "How dare you get the minister to say such things about your mother? We will not be returning to your house for drinks, we will be in touch in due course."

Returning to the funeral car the lady funeral director on opening the door for them commented,

"Bloody marvellous address by the minister, wish they had said that at my dad's funeral, he was an old bastard and they said such nice things about him at his funeral!!!"

On returning home they all felt a little deflated, food but no one to eat it!!! But then mother's neighbours and a few other folk turned up to say hello to Tigger and his family, saying very nice words of support. They certainly made them all feel a lot better. They knew the real mother Tigger had to endure for so many years.

On returning to work Tigger tried to get stuck in to learning more about the job. He had to see clients from a large client base initially accompanied by his office manager. All part of the training. As time progressed he was to work long and hard hours to establish himself as a valid member of the office team.

One morning at home, an envelope dropped through the door.

"Postman, Tigger," Wen called.

Opening it, Tigger's heart was pounding, fearful Tony would have been left most of the inheritance.

"God, she's left Tony the bungalow!!! I don't believe it!" exclaimed Tigger.

"Calm down," Wen said. "Read it again slowly to make sure you have it right."

"Ah, she's left him the bungalow, to live in, maintain and pay for all the costs of running it. She's only left him five grand, he won't be happy with that. I cannot see him wanting the bungalow to pay for all the maintenance, anyway he has his own place. Oh, there's a bit more. Ha! And when he has finished living in it or if he does not want to live in it, the bungalow is to be sold and the funds placed in trust for Andrew."

"She has left us a small amount, bit more than Tony, to Beatrice and the remainder is to be placed in trust for Andrew until he is aged 21. The trustees to be the two cousins from Leicestershire. The trust was to be an income and accumulation trust, we can use it for Andrew's education and allowable expenses, useful."

The estate had a considerable value and together with the proceeds from the sale of the bungalow would amount to a tidy sum by the time Andrew was aged 21.

Letters were exchanged between Tigger and the cousin who was the main trustee, explaining the trust but also tearing Tigger off a strip for the way he had treated his mother and what a disgrace the funeral was, with what the minister had said, obviously Tigger had instructed the Minister to say this!!! Upsetting but soon put to the back of his mind. His family was so much more important to him than some cousin who he rarely was in contact with.

Tigger and his family could now get on with their lives. A holiday to Switzerland was a reward to themselves to get over the trauma of the last few months and years, paid for by Tigger's mother, part of his inheritance!!!

Finale

Over the next few years family life was good for Tigger.

Keith excelled at university and Tigger, Wen and Andrew plus Wen's mum and an aunt went up to London for the awards ceremony. Afterwards they were shown around the university and work done by the students and of course Keith was proud to show his own work. Bearing in mind it was modern art, the aunt chirped up.

"Gosh, Keith, is that your work you did HERE? You did better when you were at play school!!!"

How they laughed.

Tigger excelled at his work with Friends Provident. He and Wendy went to company events to Zimbabwe, Borneo, Rio and the 1998 World Cup football finals, on the back of his business successes. Keith has married Steph and they live happily near Uttoxeter. Ian married Nicky and gave Tigger and Wen two lovely grandchildren, James and Jodie. Andrew qualified as a very good car mechanic.

Tigger retired early at aged 59 before work completely took over his life at the expense of his family!!! He took Wen, Andrew James, Jodie, Ian and Nicky on a once in a lifetime Christmas holiday to Lapland where they all enjoyed a winter

Wonderland with the REAL Father Christmas in a lovely log cabin in the woods!

Andrew met Gina and at 21 they went travelling for two months to Thailand and Japan to celebrate his inheritance. On their return they gave Tigger and Wen another beautiful granddaughter, Devon. They then decided to move to Spain to start a new life followed by Tigger and Wen. At the time of writing they have all been living in Spain for ten years but Tigger and Wen are hoping to return to Rustington, where their roots are and where they wish to end their days. Unfortunately Andrew and Gina parted company and Andrew is now living in England, a further reason for Tigger and Wen to return HOME! (Tigger and Wen are now back in their beloved Rustington as is Andrew in a new happy relationship—Devon remains in Spain with her mother))

I hope all who have read this book will have enjoyed the many ups and downs of Tigger's life and whilst adoption is a wonderful thing to be able to do, it does not always work out. Although Tigger had a rough time with his adoptive mother it did make him toughen up and gave him the will to succeed in whatever he did. He has since been able to trace his birth family, having met cousins and second cousins and other distant relatives who have welcomed him into the family. One family member, Mary, his mother's cousin has been particularly welcoming and has traced the family tree on his mother's side back to the early 1700s. Tigger was also able to obtain his father's full army records. He was married three times and eventually retired to Australia!!! The reason the trail went dead in Tigger's efforts to trace him!!! Tigger also went to Horse Shoe Lodge Reunions. At the first he was introduced to former residents. For them Tigger was the final piece of a jigsaw. The old house of Horseshoe Lodge had a sweeping staircase with many many photos of previous residents and Tigger was the first photo at the top of the stairs and they had never met Tigger until then. Auntie Peta had died some years previously and Mim took over the running of the house. When Mim decided enough was enough and children became fostered rather than being in a residential home Horseshoe Lodge was sold for redevelopment into a small upmarket housing estate. Mim gave Tigger a package. His record of the time he was with the Casewell Family. The package contained some very revealing information. A photo album or the early days of Tigger, letters Tigger had sent to Auntie Peta and copies of letters she had sent to Tigger's adoptive mother, which were heart wrenching. She wrote of her devastation that Tigger had been taken from her with only 24 hours' notice and that although she had two children of her own she treated Tigger as one of her own as the family had hoped one day to be in a position financially to adopt Tigger as one of her own. 'It was like having a limb torn from my body when Tigger was taken from me', she wrote. This brought Tigger and Wen to tears. Readers will recall that one of the conditions of Tigger's adoption was that he was to go to people who could provide him with a good private education. The Casewell's could not afford to do this at this time but hoped to be able to do so in the future. A month after Tigger left Horseshoe Lodge a wealthy benefactor, hearing about Tigger and the education conditions, came forward to offer all the money to provide Tigger with a lifetime of private education. Sadly it was too late, Tigger had gone. This gave Auntie Peta further heartache. Mim is still alive, not in very good health but Tigger and Wen still keep in touch.

And Tony? Well he died about three years after Tigger's mother!

Tigger dedicates this book to his adorable wife Wen who has given him so much support in life and to Cousin Mary from his REAL family. I love you ALL.

Tigger and Wen Happy in Retirement

As artificial intelligence and machine learning practices grow, entire industries and jobs could become more automated or cease to exist altogether. HR Without People traces provocative and challenging timelines for future developments in ten, thirty and fifty years' time, to interrogate how modern HR practices need to respond to far reaching technological and industrial change.

Focusing on the role these technologies are playing in changing the HR profession and how they could and should develop industry practices in the future, HR experts Anthony R. Wheeler and M. Ronald Buckley explore how this profession has a vital role in responding to these changes and how it can adapt to meet the new challenges faced by both employers and employees.

Examining key issues such as the effects of big data and algorithms ongoing role in influencing recruiting and selection, the changes in virtual technology that will alter training, and how the role of government will expand to address the needs of citizens affected by the rate of change in workforce displacement, HR without People is a stimulating and confrontational challenge to conventional thinking on this people-centric profession's role in the future of work.

ANTHONY R. WHEELER is Dean of the School of Business Administration and professor of management at Widener University. His research focuses on employee turnover and retention, employee stress, burnout, engagement, and leadership.

M. RONALD BUCKLEY is the JC Penney Company Chair of Business Leadership and a Professor of Management and a Professor of Psychology in the Price College of Business at the University of Oklahoma.

ISBN 978-1-80117-040-6

Cover
design:
Mike Hill

9 781801 170406 >

CPSIA information can be obtained
at www.ICGtesting.com
Printed in the USA
BVHW091010240122
627022BV00013B/406